WRITING WRONGS:

My Political Journey in Black and Write

BY RAYNARD JACKSON

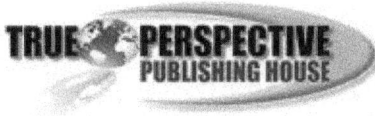

TRUE PERSPECTIVE PUBLISHING HOUSE

Writing Wrongs:
My Political Journey in Black and Write

Printed in the United States of America

ISBN - 978-0-9894026-6-8

FORWARD

I have watched Raynard grow and mature, both personally and professionally, into a person who has achieved a great deal of success; but yet remained true to his morals and values. There are many writers, pundits, and TV personalities in the marketplace; but I have yet to see or hear anyone present the perspective that I get from Raynard's writings.

As a former aide to President Richard Nixon, I understand the importance of someone who can take policy positions and put them into a language that moves the public to your viewpoint.

Of all the weapons available to a political operative, Raynard's instrument of choice is the pen. As we look back at his more than a decade of writings, one can see the growth in his writing skills and his God given ability to take an issue, internalize it, and create a column that forces you to confront an issue that challenges you to the core.
His writing is truly a gift from God and one that is needed in this world of no boundaries. He is more than a writer; he is more like a story-teller. His skills allow him to pull you into his columns, but also make it easy for you to understand complicated issues.

Even if you disagree with him, you can't help but to be drawn to his very unique perspective on issues everyone is talking about. The market-place is filled with columnists who are mostly saying the same thing. Conservative writers echoes Republican talking points; liberal writers echoes Democratic talking points.

Raynard is not the type person who fits neatly into the various boxes people try to place him in.

Growing up in St. Louis and being Black, he had no choice but to be a Democrat. But, upon his graduating from Oral Roberts University and returning home to work with Black Republicans like Curtis Crawford and Bill White he realized that his values were more in line with the Republican Party than the Democratic Party.

Who knew the relationship between Blacks and the Cadillac automobile and the role prostitutes played in saving the iconic car before his column, "The Republican Party Needs A Cadillac?" Then he masterfully connected Blacks and Cadillac to the Republican Party.

Who knew about Claudette Colvin, the first Rosa Parks, before his column, "Rosa Parks—Standing Tall by Sitting Down?"

How could you not be moved by his poetic tributes to former NBA and Jazz great, Wayman Tisdale ("Wayman Tisdale—In Memoriam"), Michael Jackson ("Ode To Michael Jackson"), or Whitney Houston ("Ode To Whitney Houston")? I didn't know Raynard had this poetic gift in him.

I have never seen a columnist who can write stinging, serious pieces, then write poetry, then inject humor into a serious piece that makes you laugh ("Heterophobia is the New Black"). Raynard has told me on many occasions that, "humor is just a funny way of being serious."

This God given ability goes to his genius as a writer. Just as soon as you think you have his writing figured out, he surprises you yet again with a totally unique take on a current event.

I have been blessed to work very personally with people like the Rev. Dr. Martin Luther King, Jr., President Nelson Mandela, and President Richard Nixon, to name a few. If Raynard was around during these times, with his skill set; he would have been viewed as one of the top political operatives in the country—Black or white, Democrat or Republican.

I look forward to reading his weekly columns and am proud to call him a friend.

Robert J. Brown
Chairman and CEO
B&C Associates, Inc. (former top aide to President Richard M. Nixon, and confidante to Nelson Mandela and Rev. Dr. Martin Luther King, Jr.).

WHAT FRIENDS ARE SAYING

"I value Raynard's friendship and his diverse and differing views. He may view me as a mentor, but I have learned much from him."

Ambassador Eric M. Javits, (ret'd), former Ambassador and Permanent U.S. Representative to the Conference on Disarmament in Geneva

Raynard Jackson is a unique individual who has been gifted in many ways, as a skillful writer with a mix of humor, compassion and honesty. When you read *Writing Wrongs* you might think Raynard is unconventional, unorthodox and controversial. His writings will leave you saying, hmmmmmmmm I never thought about that issue in that way. He provides perspectives and insights that will both excite and challenge the reader. I find his masterful work to be intellectually stimulating and thought provoking.

Danetta G. Jackson, west coast musical director

Raynard is a strong voice for the principles on which America was founded. He is a thought leader that presents reliable and well-grounded stories and concepts—influencing countless thousands of lives with his intriguing writing content and style. I appreciate his focus on research and presentation.

Ossie Mills, Executive Vice President of Advancement, Oral Roberts University

"I am not big on a lot of words, but suffice it to say that Raynard's book is a slam dunk."

Spud Webb, 13 year N.B.A. professional and 1986 N.B.A. All-Star Slam Dunk champion.

"I have known Raynard both professionally and personally for many years and marvel at his writing abilities. I look forward to reading his columns every week. If he could sing as well as he writes, he would be on stage with the rest of his brothers!"

Marlon Jackson, member of the Jackson 5

For almost 25 years, I have had a working and family relationship with Raynard. We do not always agree on his weekly message, but I respect and admire his courage. I always await his next message. His positions are current and challenges us to search beyond our own positions. Awakening!

Jose Nino, former president & CEO of the Hispanic Chamber of Commerce

"Raynard Jackson is a truth teller. It doesn't matter whether you agree with him or not, his powerful but balanced commentary makes you think and react. *Writing Wrongs* is a fascinating 10 year look at the world as Raynard sees, feels and interprets it. Always, witty, provocative and insightful, Raynard tells it like it is. This is a book well worth the money and reading it will be proven to be time well spent. Thank you Ray for 10 great years of biting commentary and journalistic leadership."

George C. Fraser, Author: Success Runs In Our Race and CLICK

"Raynard's monograph is incisive, like a surgeon's scalpel; sharp, at times painful and cathartic, but always instructive and insightful."

Edwin J. Wang, Managing Partner, Accretive Capital Partners.

Raynard has not ever been one for mincing words or biting his tongue. As a high school student in my accounting class, he was known for thoughtfully analyzing and considering each situation before expressing an opinion that provoked further thought and more often than not—much debate. Calling out the "elephant in the room" has never been a problem for him and has been reflected in his writing throughout the years. His conversations and writings require one to stretch and to go beyond current comfort zones by considering other realities and possibilities rather than accepting the status quo of unchallenged ideas. Writing Wrongs: My Political Journey in Black and Write represents Raynard at his provocative best!

Betty H. Tobler, Retired Teacher and Administrator, Saint Louis Public Schools

"Raynard has always been willing to challenge the status quo, even within his own party. The world needs more people who dare to be different." *Roland S. Martin, Host/Managing Editor, News One Now, TV One Cable Network*

Raynard Jackson is an amazingly gifted writer, narrator, and political thinker. This book encompasses life through the lens of a conservative African American thought leader. His writings are provocative, raw, authentic, and forward thinking. I invite you to read, engage, and become color-blind.

K. David Boyer, Jr., CEO, GlobalWatch Technologies

"Raynard Jackson brings his distinctive, American perspective to any subject or issue he addresses. I invariably come away having learned something new or re-examined my own opinion."

Leora R. Levy, very dear friend

INTRODUCTION

The purpose of this book is not to convert my readers into Republicans, but rather to share some of my columns where I have taken a stand on specific issues.

I don't write about salacious subject matters—there are many other outlets for that. I prefer to write about current events and give insightful analysis that is not currently being presented to readers.

My goal is not to convince my readers to agree with me, but rather to get them to be willing to think a "new" thought. You can disagree with me, but as long as I caused you to rethink your position on a given issue; then my goal has been accomplished.

For example, how many of you know the connection between Blacks and the Cadillac automobile? How many of you know why the Civil Rights community chose Rosa Parks to be the face of the movement? How many of you are familiar with Tony McGee and the Wyoming 14?

In this book, you will find the answer to these questions. The answers will cause you to rethink how you view each of those subject matters.

That is my goal with this book—to stretch your mind to a new dimension.

TABLE OF CONTENTS

PROLOGUE

I have been writing newspaper columns for almost ten years and have been syndicated by the National Newspaper Publishers Association (NNPA) for more than a year.

My columns have been published in news outlets from the Washington Post, Fox News, The Root-DC, Politics 365, AOL Black Voices, and Charisma Magazine, The Washington Informer, The New Pittsburgh Courier, The Sacramento Observer, The Atlanta Daily World, and Afro-American Newspaper of Washington, DC, etc.

I am not a journalist, but rather a writer. My writing skills were perfected by three of my high school teachers back at Soldan High School in St. Louis, MO.

Mrs. Bobbie Clay, Ethel Hughes, and Brian Cox made me in to the writer I am today, especially Mr. Cox. I took an honors English class with him and he was probably the toughest teacher ever known to mankind. I am sure my fellow Soldan alumni will attest to this.

As a result of these three teacher's constantly prodding me to be better, I have been able to master the art of writing; but, through my insatiable thirst for knowledge and my curiosity about life, I have merged my writing skills with my creativity.

My writing skills and my global travels have been the driving forces behind my unique voice within the world of opinion writing.

My purpose is not to get people to agree with me, but rather to compel my readers to think outside of their comfort zones.

During the past few years people have asked me where they could find a compilation of my columns. Since there was no one place to find my writings, it was suggested that I compile some of my best columns into a book. Thus the impetus for, "Writing Wrongs: My Political Journey in Black and Write."

CHAPTER 1

❦ POETRY ❧

INTRODUCTION BY:

Marcus R. Johnson, NAACP Image Award Nominee for "Poetically Justified," Billboard Contemporary Jazz Artist Top 20, and CEO Flo Brands, LLC/Flo Wine Inc.

Raynard Jackson is a thought provoking columnist who looks at politics and the plight of America and African Americans through the eyes of hope. I have always admired his courage to be on the front lines of African American conservatism. While others speak and write of hope - yet stay in a land of comfort - Raynard has taken Robert Frost's "Road Less Traveled!" It cannot be easy working as an African American who holds socially and financially conservative views. However, in the face of a structural bias toward Black Democratic Liberalism, Raynard publicly posits a different lens through which all can ponder the plight of contemporary African Americanism.

Raynard is an advocate for black business in the US and abroad and works tirelessly to connect small business with those around the world without regard to political views. This quality is even more considerate when one understands our dichotomous existence in the US. In other words, he thinks. Raynard gives his readers the truth, unvarnished. He equally challenges both conservatives and liberals on issues that he feels strongly about. Raynard is very passionate about his views, but never intolerant of those who might disagree with him.

As a Georgetown University trained lawyer, I feel that this is how it should be. Everyone is entitled to their view. Everyone is entitled to their beliefs. But Raynard has a way of challenging your core beliefs that is very powerful. What separates Raynard from his fellow columnists is his ability to inject creativity and humor into his writing. This is truly a gift from God. This section on poetry is very creative, but yet his message is very stinging. In the midst of writing about a somber event, he is warm and embracing.

In music, it's like being able to go from Jazz to R & B, to Blues, but yet stay within yourself. I know from personal experience as a professional musician, that you are either born with this gift or you are not. You can't teach this. This is a gift from God. I congratulate Raynard on his book and hope you are ready for an intellectually engaging experience.

Letter to Dr. King

Published: Jan. 31, 2005

Y ou didn't know me when you were here,
But through your words I feel you are near.

I was too young for the demonstration,
But I learned about you in my education.

You said we all were created equal,
But, maybe now we need a new sequel.

Because I don't know what happened to the dream,
Nor the members of your team.

Yeah, Andy's made a name,
Jesse got some fame.

But what happened to the vision?
Seems it's been lost to indecision.

Do we continue to blame whites for our plight,
'Cause it's easier than to stand and fight?

Do we need integration to survive?
We did pretty good without it, to my surprise.

Should we attend college at an HBCU,
Or, go to Harvard, Princeton or even Purdue?

You said we should not be judged by the color of our skin,
Does that apply to the political party I'm in?

Some ask me, "How can you be Black and Republican?"
Because, like you Dr. King, I believe in the "I CAN."

You were invited to the White House for conversation,
Because everyone saw your dedication.

Now we call the president bad for Blacks,
But, look at how these leaders act.

They call him evil and a racist man,
Though his cabinet shows he understands.

Did you ever dream of a Black secretary of state?
We've come a long way from that era of hate.

Did you dream of a Black national security advisor?
Maybe white folks have gotten a little wiser.

To put Blacks in a position where a lot fail,
Because most of the time we excel.

Lenny Wilkens in the NBA,
DeWayne Wickam at USA Today.

Barack Obama in the Senate,
Ran because he thought he could win it.

Dr. Ben Carson with the knife,
Saves life after life.

But how did we come to this place,
Where we now curse our own race?

Rappers call our women bitches and ho's,
Where it will stop, God only knows.

Our teenagers are committing crimes,
And getting locked up for a helluva long time.

Who is there to show them the light,
'Cause their fathers are nowhere in sight.

So our women accept living with anger,
Which is only one letter short of danger.

I have kept my nose clean and finished school,
But, I am becoming the exception to the rule.

Marriage before kids is how I was raised,
Why are women so amazed?

Having a family is a serious thing,
No kids without a wedding ring.

We have allowed drugs to devastate our lives,
Preachers, where are your righteous cries?

We have cursed Bill Cosby's name,
When he should be in our hall of fame.

Dr. King, please explain your dream,
I am not sure if it's what it seems.

Everyone is now invoking your name,
Just to get political gain.

Some say you would be for gay rights,
Was that really part of the fight?

Some say you would be Republican or Democrat,
But neither is borne out by the facts.

You just wanted the powers that be to be accountable,
Because back then, the mountain seemed so
insurmountable.

We have more education in our head,
But, more of our people are ending up dead.

We have more freedom to move around,
But, our quality of life seems to be going down.

Among our people are so many divisions,
Whatever happened to your heavenly vision?

Dr. King, if you were here today,
I would be ashamed of what you would say.

We have strayed so far from the path.
How much longer can this stuff last?

We must get back to the dream,
But, please tell us what does it mean?

President Barack Obama

Published: January 22, 2009

Now that we had inauguration day,
I have something I want to say.
Let's take a look back at history,
And try to unravel a wonderful mystery.

Now that Obama is President,
I know he will represent,
The great red, white and Blue,
That includes me and that includes you.

They said it could not be done,
Why in the hell would he run?
Is this boy crazy or lost his mind?
He just knew that now was the time.

To put a new agenda on the table,
Then to make it happen because he was able.
To create a new vision and give people hope.

Even when people said he must be on dope.

Rush, Sean, and Laura called him an elite,
They said he would surely face defeat.
They even called him the Messiah,
Even as his poll numbers climbed higher.

The Clinton machine, he could never beat,
But he proved to be quick on his feet.
Never, ever raising his voice,
Because he knew he was the people's choice.

The choice of a new generation,
To create a spirit of inspiration.
Not just because he wanted to win this race,
But to tell all Americans you have a place.

In getting us back to our original glory,
And his victory would only be the beginning of the story.
A story of the growth of a nation,
Whose worst moment was symbolized by the plantation.

We moved from the plantation,
To a nation of appreciation.
For the determination of a race,
Who constantly struggled to find its place.

Then came a man who said Yes We Can,
But first, there must be a plan.
So people could see the vision,
He became the vessel to end the division.

Now that he is President, the job is not done,
This work has only just begun.
We can all be part of the dream,
By making our contribution to the team.

He is only one man,
But was the voice of the plan.
But we all must understand,
That only together **"YES WE CAN!"**

Wayman Tisdale- In Memoriam

Published: May 21, 2009

L ast Friday, I received the shocking news of the sudden death of my good friend, Wayman Tisdale. Tisdale played basketball for 3 years at Oklahoma University and 12 years in the N.B.A. (Indiana, Sacramento, and Phoenix).

Upon retiring from basketball, he went on to have a critically acclaimed music career as a jazz bassist. He recorded a total of 8 CDs beginning in 1995 ("Power Forward" on the Motown Label). His last CD, Rebound (2008), was written and released during his recovery from cancer. He was scheduled to be in the studio this week to work on his next CD.

I had known Wayman for many years. We first met when I was a student at Oral Roberts University in Tulsa, Oklahoma. His father was pastor of a very prominent church there and many O.R.U. students attended his church.

Wayman was a tall, but not yet imposing figure. He played bass guitar for the church. His hands were huge. We called him "thunder thumbs" because of his hand size and the way he plucked his guitar. He was left handed, but always played a right handed bass (he turned the guitar upside down).

We lost contact with each other after I left O.R.U., but we reconnected several years ago at one of his concerts. It was one of the best concerts I have ever been to. Wayman was a wild and crazy guy and he acted the same when he was on stage. He was so wild that he made me look like an introvert (and that's not easy to do)!

During my radio show last Saturday, I spent 30 minutes paying tribute to Wayman's life with a good friend (and former teammate of Wayman's), Spud Webb.

In the midst of this tragedy, I am heartened by all the kind words expressed about Wayman and his life. From the governor of Oklahoma, teammates, the N.B.A., etc.

You can't talk about Wayman without mentioning his smile! No matter how bad your day was or how bad you were feeling, when Wayman came around, you were going to end up smiling—if not laughing.

Wayman was born to be happy. He was born to make others happy. In August of last year, he had his right leg amputated above the knee. Just imagine, a professional athlete losing a leg. Wayman was 6'9" and 240 pounds and now needing help to get around. I work with a lot of professional athletes and all have said the same thing about Wayman—that he was a special person to handle his sickness like he did. Most of us would have become totally despondent in a similar situation.

Could it be that Wayman was born for such a time like this? In his death his spirit will live on, especially when we go through our personal trials and tribulations. Those who knew Wayman will be able to draw strength from his life.

Wayman played **"Power Forward"** and when he was **"In The Zone"** he made his best **"Decisions."** After **"Face to Face,"** he **"Presents 21 Days,"** his first gospel CD. He proved to the industry that he had **"Hang Time"** when his sales went **"Way Up!"** In the last chapter of his life he showed that he could **"Rebound"** from his cancer diagnosis.

But, I am still having problems accepting that Wayman is gone so soon. I have pondered what would Wayman say or do. These are the words that popped into my head: "O, death where is thy sting? O grave, where is thy victory? For death has been swallowed up in victory."

Wayman, you indeed have won the ultimate game of life. You played your heart out. It's OK, **"It's Alright,"** 'cause you never gave up the fight. You have left us for a while, but you did leave us with the lasting image of your great big smile.

Ode to Michael Jackson

Published: July 2, 2009

L
ike a candle in the wind,
Your life came to a sudden end.
With **"A Child's Heart,"**
You began your start.

You brought joy to many,
But in the end, you didn't have any.
You had money, fortune, and fame,
If that's all we remember, what a shame.

Now, they all say, **"I Want You Back,"**
But is that all just an act?
They all said, **"I'll Be There,"**
I am not sure they really care.

While you were making your journey home,
Sharpton was already in front of the microphone.
Trying to bask in your glorious light,
Doing that just wasn't right.

Standing in front of the Apollo,
This stunt rang really hollow.
Grandstanding in front of the press,
My goodness, such a pathetic mess.

I thought Obama had silenced Jesse Jackson,
But, I guess he was just waiting for the next media attraction.
Come on Jesse, start being a man,
And just stay away from Neverland.

Now, Al and Jesse are fighting over the eulogy,
Not even death can bring them unity.
I am sickened by their behavior,
Yet they claim Jesus as their savior.

The media is airing all sorts of speculation,
None of it proven is my observation.
I am embarrassed by their actions,
They're just trying to use Michael Jackson.

Airing anyone who claims to have a story,

All the while, trying to diminish Michael's glory.

Why in the world is the media so hating?

I guess they're just trying to increase their ratings.

Some say you lived your life **"Off The Wall,"**

But, who are we to make that call?

Yes, you had your eccentricities,

But that shouldn't overshadow what a man believes.

You tried to do good with your voice,

And became the people's choice.

The choice of a whole generation,

And they gave you their total adulation.

You saw a world that was not **Black or White,**

Because **Healing the World**, was worth the fight.

You challenged us to look at that **"Man In The Mirror,"**

So your vision of unity could become clearer.

You wanted gangs to start uniting,

Songs like **"Beat It"** helped them stop fighting.

You didn't have to prove you were **"Bad,"**

You just talked about the childhood you never had.

You were put on this earth to be a blessing to many,

Now everyone is going to be fighting for every penny,

What will be the true legacy of your life?
It's hard to see in the midst of all this strife.

You had the best friends money could buy,
Guess that's why I see no tears in their eye.
Other friends were the best you could rent,
I pray one day they'll repent.

Catherine Jackson, you are a saint,
With you, Michael never had a complaint.
I hope you are surrounded with those who care,
If not, just call my name and **"I'll Be There!"**

The State of the Dream

Published: August 25, 2011

With all the attention being focused on the life and legacy of the Rev. Dr. Martin Luther King, Jr. this week, I have been pondering what he would have to say about the state of his legacy. In the immortal words of Lionel Richie (former lead singer of the Commodores):

"I may be just a foolish dreamer but I don't care,
Cause I know my happiness is waiting out there somewhere.

I'm searching for that silver lining,
Horizons that I've never seen.
Oh I'd like to take just a moment and dream my dream,
Oooh, dream my dream" (from the song Zoom1977).

I can imagine King looking down from on high and
observing the state of his dream:

What the hell has become of my dream?
Nothing is what it really seems.
My people have been emancipated, but yet are not free,
Just look at the high rate of poverty.

My people have better education,
But they also exhibit less dedication.
Their thirst for material possessions,
Seems to be their only obsession.

The Martin Luther King, Jr. National Memorial Project,
Let the record show I totally object.
To spend $ 120 million and to what end?
That's not what the dream was about my friend.

Lei Yixin, the sculptor that was chosen,
When I found out, my mouth was frozen.
A man from China where there are no human rights,
You can believe I would have put up a big fight!

$ 800,000 to my family for the use of my name,
Yolanda, Marty, Dexter, and Bernice what a shame.
Yeah, I know there is money in intellectual property,
But, my dream was always more towards the heavenly.

A German to build a memorial to the Holocaust?
The Jewish community would have been at a loss.
But my people gave the work to a non American,
This oddity I really can't understand.

You couldn't have chosen someone like the sculptor Ed
Dwight?
After all, the U.S. Air Force trusted him to take planes into
flight.

A Black man trained as a sculptor, aviator and an
aeronautical engineer,
His choice should have been crystal clear.

Getting the raw materials from a foreign land,
To build the platform on which I stand.
From China of all places, a repressive regime,
This choice makes me want to scream!

Temporary workers from China you brought to this land,
What, there were no American workers skilled with their
hands?
No doubt this was all about cheap wages,
This has been man's downfall throughout the ages.

Oh, and what's this I hear about the granite brought in
from China?

You couldn't find any in North Carolina?
Has my dream really come down to this?
I thought by now there would be a new twist.

When I left earth to take my rest,
I thought my people could pass the test.
Now, as I look down on this situation,
I wish I could have one more incarnation.

But, who am I to question what God has started?
Maybe that's why I am a member of the dearly departed.
I now wish I could have one more run,
But my fate was tied to the barrel of a gun.

So, as I leave you with these final words,
I hope the true meaning of my vision is what you heard.
I am not allowed to come back and continue the fight,
So, please try to get my dream right.

I will pray that God will open your eyes,
Because what I see is a stunning surprise.
The dream was not about the money spent,
But helping those who could barely pay their rent.

Yes, it's true that the dream was for all of mankind,
But, what I see you doing is not what I had in mind.
My dream was not about the color of the skin,

But, tell me where does the Black man fit in?

But, giving contracts to those from a foreign nation,
Was not part of my dream of emancipation?
Everything for this project could have come from within
Please understand what I am saying to you my friend.

ODE TO WHITNEY HOUSTON

Published: February 23, 2012

Whitney, as you began to take your heavenly journey,
We all saw a picture of you on a medical gurney.
Then all kinds of thoughts flooded into my head,
Because I knew many things were about to be said.

The show must go on they all said,
While they were partying, you laid dead.
All sorts of people began invoking your name,
This seemed more about cashing in on your fame.

Kelly Price was all over CNN,
Was that the best way to remember your friend?

Every time I turned around,
On another network she could be found.

CNN's Don Lemon was almost in tears,
Saying your music had touched his life for years.
My, my, my, what a difference a day makes,
Because the next day he had quite a different take.

He began rampant speculation on your cause of death,
Your spirit, from your body had barely left.
He claimed you had such a heavenly voice,
But, the tools of speculation were his journalistic choice.

So-called friends who were with you days before,
Have turned into such media whores.
Before your body was placed in the ground,
All over TV they could be found.

To the media, do you know no shame?
Even in death, it's all just a game.
It's all about ratings and making money,
But, when it happens to your family it won't be so funny.

To the media, public figures are mere sport,
Calling an 18 year old child they did resort.
Bobbi Christina doesn't deserve this type of attention,
So, why in your stories is she even mentioned?

Though Whitney had her own demons to bear,
In her death she was treated so unfair.
When you look at her life as a whole,
She seemed to be such a beautiful soul.

Cissy, no parent should have to bury a child,
But, you will see her again after a while.
You have handled this situation with class and grace,
I pray God will continue to shine his favor upon your face.

Cissy, Whitney's home going celebration,
Filled my heart with great jubilation.
You only had Whitney for 48 years,
So I understand why your eyes filled with tears.

That's such a short time in the big scheme of things,
But just think of how many hearts she made to sing.
God gave you that gift of song,
This gift will help you to be strong.

Stevie, isn't it amazing that love's still in need of love,
Alicia, you are that angel from above.
The way you sang that song it was very clear,
That Whitney was someone you held very dear.

But, then there was another side to this event,
A side that had an ugly bent.

One person made me so furious,
Why he behaved so, I'm just curious.

Could Al Sharpton not watch and pray?
Why would he send out tweets while your funeral was underway?
Could he not sit there and show his respects,
As long as he got in the media, he figured what the heck?

Maybe he was angry because he was not asked to speak,
So, other ways to get into the media he did seek.
Al, I can't take you anymore,
You are the biggest media whore.

You claimed in your tweet you told Bobby Brown not to be a distraction,
But then you became one by your very action.
Tweeting during Whitney's funeral was a classless act,
But, then again, your history of this type of behavior is a known fact.

Whitney deserved her one moment in time,
Sharpton, your behavior was such a selfish crime.
Do you see no shame in upstaging the dead?
Maybe next time you should use your heart, not your head.

Whitney, now that you have completed your journey, may
you be at rest
For 48 years you gave us your best.
Though you were an icon all over the world,
To Cissy, you were just her little girl.

CHAPTER 2

❦ CULTURE ❦

INTRODUCTION BY:

Sean Moss, Principal, Kardia Partners (and former Regional Director for U.S. Housing and Urban Development for President George W. Bush).

In a world like today, it's rare to find a columnist who will take a strong, principled stand regarding our seeming degradation of our American culture. We seem to be spiraling out of control all in the name of freedom, tolerance and diversity.

Raynard has made it perfectly clear that he supports and agrees with the principles regarding freedom, tolerance and diversity; but he has also made it clear that these issues must be coupled with the issue of responsibility.

Rights are what we are given by our constitution as an American citizen. Responsibility is what we give back to our fellow Americans as a citizen.

Raynard tackles controversial issues like: illegal immigration, homosexuality, God in the public square, and the liberal media bias. Whether you agree with him or not, Raynard has proven in his writings that he is a traditionalist when it comes to values. A traditionalist believes in the rule of law, right and wrong, and accountability for one's actions.

Today, Americans are only obsessed with their rights; not their responsibilities, which make rights possible. This symbiotic relationship between rights and responsibilities lead to values that are the glue that binds a society together. Some would argue that Raynard's values are antiquated, but he challenges us to rethink the relationship between values and responsibility. Out of control crime, out of wedlock children, lack of respect for elders are all derivatives of America's obsession with rights devoid of responsibility.

He argues that you can't legislate values and morality—it must be driven by society. You can legislate gun ownership, you can get rid of food stamps, and you can outlaw all drugs; but until you deal with the heart of a man, none of these issues will go away.

It is refreshing to read Raynard's columns where he takes a very definite position on some of the most controversial issues of our day. Even those who disagree with him have trouble refuting his arguments.

In many ways, Raynard is way ahead of his time. I am astonished at some of the things he wrote years in advance only to see them become reality. His insight is almost prophetic and I would consider him one of the cultural prophets of our day. If you are open to being intellectually challenged, then this book was written for you.

An Annual Tavisty

Published: February 23, 2005

Once again we come to the time of the year where radical liberal Blacks begin their annual pilgrimage to beat up on white folks and Republicans. Of course I am making reference to Tavist Smiley & Tom Joyner's annual "complaining session" about what white folks are not doing for Blacks and how Republicans are responsible for all the social pathologies in our community. It begins around King's birthday, continues through Black history month, and culminates with the Congressional Black Caucus's annual party.

As if that wasn't bad enough, Smiley and Joyner have invited as their speakers the usual cast of characters: Cornell West (professor at Princeton), Marian Wright

Edelman, The Children's Defense Fund, Julian Bond, NAACP, Theodore Shaw, NAACP Legal Defense and Educational Fund, Jesse Jackson, Sr., Rainbow/PUSH Coalition, Harry Belafonte, Actor & Activist, Bishop Eddie L. Long, Congresswoman Maxine Waters, etc., to name a few.

What do all these have in common? They are all radical liberals with no new ideas. Name me ANY issue and I will tell you their response because they are so predictable.

Let's assume for the sake of this discussion, that we could magically snap our fingers and all white folks disappeared. How would that change the fact that Black kids watch more TV than any other group, that Black women are graduating more from college than our males, that Black girls continue to have out of wedlock births at an alarming rate, for those who go to college, they are studying subjects with no future job demand (Black studies).

The tragedy behind Tavist's annual complaint session is that in our community, there is a wealth of ideas and views; but Mr. Smiley only assembles those who are like minded. When you are seeking solutions to devastating problems, friendships and like ideologies is not the answer. We must tap into the brilliance that our people have shown throughout history.

Even though there were Malcolm and Martin wings of the civil rights movement, for the most part, both factions made positive contributions to the struggle. There were the Washington-Dubois factions, but again they both contributed to the cause.

We must not isolate any group that has positive solutions to contribute to our community, be it Black or white, Democrat or Republican. There's too much at stake!

I challenge Black Voices (BV) members to name me one tangible thing that has come as a result of Tavist's annual complaint session (or any of the similar meetings that take place annually in our community). You will have over 10,000 people to attend this event and to what avail?

These annual gatherings from Tavis, the Congressional Black Caucus, and the N.A.A.C.P. must stop if they are going to remain devoid of substance. They have become like sounding brass or a tinkling cymbal full of sound and fury signifying nothing.

It's Time to Clean House

Published: March 9, 2005

I 've said this all before. Last year, when Kweisi Mfume announced he would no longer preside over the NAACP, I explained in my very first column for AOL Black Voices that the NAACP was being held in bondage by its board chairman Julian Bond.

I reminded Black Voices (BV) members that despite the scandal that plagued the organization with Ben Chavis at the helm, the corporate and political communities remained committed to the group solely because of Mfume's stature.

But as the years went by, Mfume spent more of his time fighting with Bond about toning down his vitriolic rhetoric than cleaning up the mess that resulted from Bonds verbal barrages.

"The NAACP's membership is stagnant, its image sullied by Bond, its relationship with corporate America is weak and now the group has lost Mfume, its most credible leader," I wrote. "It's time for Bond to resign his position as chairman of the board and to cut all ties to the organization."

Now, let's fast forward two months. The headline in the February 20, 2005, edition of the Baltimore Sun reads: "NAACP reports a shortfall in budget at annual meeting, Baltimore headquarters has had to restructure some staff positions."

I warned that corporate America would begin to pull back its support of the NAACP, and that membership would continue to decline. Anybody could have seen this coming.

Mfume saw it, and he didn't want to have his reputation and image ruined. After many failed attempts to silence Bond, he became frustrated and got out.

Now, the organization is at a serious crossroad. It's very survival is at stake. They are having serious problems finding a replacement for Mfume. There are not many people with stature or credibility willing to head an organization that has an uncontrollable ego maniac as its chairman, the IRS auditing their activities and an almost $5 million deficit. This makes me wonder whether the

NAACP is an organization that black America still needs. Has it lost its relevance?

We are notorious for keeping old pants hanging around the house long after they are no longer useful. In most cases, they will stay in our closet until a girlfriend (boyfriend, husband, wife, mother or father) comes in and just throws them out. Does the NAACP have someone willing to clean house? They have more than 50 people on the board of directors. Managing any organization with that many people involved is impossible. I think the board should be reduced to no more than nine people, but this would hit at the very heart of their irrational management style; board seats are handed out as a way to keep people involved, even when most of the people on the board bring nothing of value to the management of the organization.

During the past couple of years, the NAACP has become increasingly less relevant. Just because we have some emotional or sentimental value associated with something doesn't justify its continued existence. Sometimes, we need to have someone "clean house." Who will do it for the NAACP by calling for Julian Bond's immediate resignation and a total overhaul of its board of directors?

God is able....But?

Published: February 11, 2009

What an amazing year thus far! Obama's inauguration, Mike Tomlin's Steelers win the Super Bowl (the youngest Black coach in the .N.F.L. and the youngest coach to win a Super Bowl in history), and Michael Steele's election as the first Black to lead the Republican Party. God has brought us from a mighty long way.

As I reflected on how far we have come, I wondered what would happen if God said, "ENOUGH." I have done all I am going to do for you. I have equipped you with everything you need to solve all your problems. I gave you brains, determination, and the heart of a lion.

What if Obama's administration doesn't do all that we wish and hope for? What if white folks or "the man" says no more equality or government programs?

Most of us are familiar with the story of Shadrach, Meshach and Abednego from the book of Daniel in the Bible. It is the story about how these three boys refused to worship the idol god of King Nebuchadnezzar. The king had issued a decree that whoever did not bow down and worship his idol would be sentenced to immediate death. Daniel 3:16-18 says: ..."O Nebuchadnezzar, we are not careful to answer thee in this matter. If it be so, our God whom we serve is able to deliver us from the burning fiery furnace, and he will deliver us out of thine hand, O king. But if not, be it known unto thee, O king, that we will not serve thy gods, nor worship the golden image which thou hast set up."

These boys had such a strong belief in God and what they believed that they knew God had the absolute power to deliver them from death. But they said even if God didn't deliver them, they would not compromise their beliefs. Our community once believed this strongly in Godly values that would not allow us to condone the behavior going on within our community today. We didn't need a bunch of government programs and handouts.

What if there is no welfare? What are we going to do as a community?   When will we return stigma to out of marriage child bearing?

What if there are no reentry programs for those leaving penal institutions? When will families and churches take them in with some tough love and get them back on their feet?

What if there is no more affirmative action? When will parents, preachers, and teachers tell students they just have do better and be better?

What if there is no justice, but only just-us? When will our community demand that our people never get caught up in the justice system?

We know there are many things the government and society should do to help its people, but the lack of governmental or societal action is no excuse for the behavior that is destroying our community. We have had more than a generation of excuses and finger pointing about what ails our community.

We can talk forever about slavery and racism. These are not the causes of out of wedlock babies, high divorce rates, drug selling, drug usage, violent crime, domestic violence, or child abuse.

Most often people are making bad decisions because they have no fear of any consequences. Spanking is considered abuse. Now we have time-outs. Parents are now afraid of their own kids. We have baby showers for pregnant teenage girls. Parents now side with their kids against the teacher.

I find it quite interesting that our parents and grandparents didn't have a lot of programs, but yet they were able to minimize all these pathologies. They had less opportunity, less education, and less information than we have. Yet, they led a better quality of life than we are today. They bought homes, cars, and put us through school, but we are self-destructing.

We have people under 30 who are grandparents. We have teenagers who have never been inside a church. We have parents trying to breed the next Michael Jordan, Tiger Woods, and Venus & Serena Williams. Children are being robbed of their childhoods by narcissistic parents.

There are no government programs that can resolve these issues. The solutions lie within us and our community. Only tough love can solve these issues. Tough love from grandparents, parents, and the community. Then and only then can programs work.

We know God is able, but......?

The God in Good

Published: April 30, 2009

There is so much negative in our world that sometime we forget about the good that is all around and the God that is in good.

A few weeks ago I was asked by Isaiah Washington (of Grey's Anatomy fame) to help him with a fundraising dinner for his foundation, The Gondobay Manga Foundation. He established the foundation to help the people of Sierra Leone in West Africa. The dinner was held last week in Washington, DC and I was glad to play a small part.

Isaiah has a true passion for Sierra Leone specifically and people in general. He had several of his Hollywood friends in attendance at the dinner who added a great deal to the event. I had the chance to meet and talk with Forest Whitaker. Forest is a very imposing figure, but surprisingly, he is very humble and soft spoken. There was a gentleness to him that draws you to him. I have always been a big fan of his and anything he is associated with, I will support. His support for Isaiah and The Gondobay Manga Foundation was very self-evident.

Another friend of Isaiah's that I met and talked with was actor Jeffry Wright. Again, another very humble person. He reminds me of a junior James Earl Jones with his distinctive voice that makes you hang on to every word he says.

Washington Wizard's center, Etan Thomas was also in attendance. A very soft-spoken person until he touches the microphone. He is just as known for reciting his original poetry as he is for his basketball skills. Now, how cool is that, a professional athlete who has social consciousness voiced through poetic prose. Look for big things from him away from basketball.

It was once said that one measure of a man is the caliber of people who choose to associate with you. By that standard, Isaiah is truly a very generous, decent person. People willing to fly across the country to attend his wonderful event was a true sign of their commitment to Isaiah and his foundation. He even had Sara Ferguson, the Duchess of York, as his keynote speaker.

I have been fortunate enough to attend some of the most elegant, high powered dinners across this country, but this one was one of the best by far. Yes, we had a worthy cause, but just as important was the caliber of people who were in attendance. I am not talking about the VIPs, but regular people who cared about this particular cause.

Sometimes events with celebrities can be kind of "uppity." But, at this event everyone mingled and interacted with one another and there was just a sweet spirit throughout the evening. So, the next time you hear negative things about Hollywood or professional athletes; just think of the heart of Isaiah Washington, the gentleness and humility of Forest Whitaker, the oratory of Jeffrey Wright or the quiet poetry of Etan Thomas.

Over the next few weeks, I hope to have each of these people on my radio show to talk about the journeys taken to get them to the level of success they have achieved. I want to explore the heart of Isaiah and why he has a passion for Sierra Leone. I want Forest to allow me to understand his path to humility. I want Jeffry to describe his road less traveled. I want Etan to share the source of his quiet voice. Sometimes in sitting, we can stand tall. I want me and my listeners to sit at each of these people's feet and learn of their ways.

This was a wonderful event for a good cause. So, I strongly encourage everyone to remember that there is a lot of good in the world and a lot of people are doing good things. So, please support Isaiah's Gondobay Manga Foundation. Support Forest's and Jeffrey's movies and TV shows. Take the time and write the heads of movie and TV studios about their work and let these executives know that you want to see more work from these talented actors. Make the commitment to buy Etan's book of poetry titled "More Than an Athlete: Poems by Etan Thomas."

So, next time you are fed up with Paris Hilton, Lindsay Lohan, Pacman Jones, or Terrell Owens; think of Isaiah, Forest, Jeffrey and Etan. Just because you didn't hear about the event, doesn't mean it didn't happen. Just because you don't hear about these celebrities charitable work, doesn't mean they are not doing it. And just because your life may not be going good at present doesn't mean God is not good.

100 Years of the NAACP—Past It's Prime

Published: July 16, 2009

As the National Association for the Advancement of Colored People (NAACP) meets this week to celebrate its 100th anniversary, I am very conflicted. First, I want to congratulate them on their first 75 years. They did a marvelous job at a time when America needed a lot of nudging down the road towards equality. Their past 25 years, however, has not been so glorious.

After 100 years, I think it's time to ponder whether this organization is still relevant. I say, it's time to bury them because they no longer represent the vision of their founders. They have devolved into a stagnant group that is more focused on hyperbole, rather than substance. One definition of a great organization is one that makes itself increasingly unnecessary. The NAACP has done just the opposite. They have fostered an atmosphere of dependency among the less fortunate.

Like a human who has 100 years, the NAACP is moving very slowly, talks a lot about the past, but refuses to contemplate whether they can thrive in this brave new world. In the day, they fought for equality and full compliance to the constitution. Now, they are involved and support everything from gay marriage, expanded welfare programs and amnesty for illegals!

What I find amazing about their position on illegal immigration is the fact that the Hispanic community (specifically the Cuban) supports discrimination against people of color, especially Haitians.

Remember the "wet foot, dry foot policy? This was a policy stemming from the 1995 revision of the Cuban Adjustment Act of 1966. The change basically states that a Cuban caught on the waters between the two nations would be sent home or to a third country. But one who makes it to shore gets a chance to remain in the U.S. and later would qualify for expedited "legal permanent resident" status and U.S. citizenship. This was put in place by the "first Black president," Bill Clinton.

But, a Haitian in a similar situation get sent immediately back to Haiti. No hope of staying in the U.S. and no hope of citizenship. When I ask pro-amnesty Hispanics about their willingness to work with me on reversing the wet foot, dry foot policy if I supported their amnesty agenda, they all have said emphatically, "**NO!**"

So, again I ask how can the NAACP continue to allow itself to be used in such a manner? Furthermore, low skilled Black workers are the ones most hurt by this amnesty proposal. I can't imagine the "old" NAACP leadership allowing themselves to be pimped in such a manner.

Sometimes, the longer an organization exists, they sometimes begin to drift away from their mission. The NAACP is a classic example of this all too common trend. Most of their funding comes from white corporations. There is nothing inherently wrong with that, but what does that say about the NAACP when the Black community won't put their own dollars behind this group?

I will **NEVER** make a contribution to the NAACP as long as Julian Bond (Chairman of the Board of the NAACP) is associated with the group! His language towards former president Bush was beneath a person of his stature. In 2001, Bond said, "Instead of uniting us, the new administration almost daily separates and divides. They selected nominees from the Taliban wing of American politics, appeased the wretched appetites of the extreme right wing and chose Cabinet officials whose devotion to the Confederacy is nearly canine in its uncritical affection."

Other statements made by Bond, "The Republican Party would have the American flag and the swastika flying side by side." There are plenty of areas of disagreement with the former president, but this language is embarrassing and unacceptable. But, Bond conveniently omitted the fact that Bush appointed more Blacks to key positions than even Bill Clinton. So, by his own measurements, Bill Clinton was a racist! So, as long as the NAACP is run by the likes of Julian Bond, don't count on my support in any form!

During the last 25 years of the group's existence, it has been run by the most liberal of liberals. When they decided to appoint Bruce Gordon as its head in 2005, I thought the group finally "got it!" Boy, was I wrong.

Gordon was the first and only head of the NAACP with a business background. He was a high ranking executive with Verizon (telephone company) and served on the board of some of the best known companies in the U.S. It was as a direct result of Gordon's shifting focus and reasonable tone that prompted then president Bush to accept his invitation to speak at their national convention (July 20, 2006).

Up to that point, Bush had refused to meet or speak to the group because of Bond's involvement. Everyone knows that the NAACP is a vestige of the Democratic National Committee (DNC).

Gordon's appointment created a positive buzz throughout corporate America. Unfortunately, Gordon only lasted less than two years as head of the group. Gordon was a "man" and would not let Bond or the other board members interfere in the day to day operations of his administration. This created immediate conflict with Bond.

So, in March of 2007 Gordon resigned his position. He basically said he didn't need this headache. Corporate donations dried up immediately. According to Gordon, "I did not step into the role to be a caretaker, to be dictated to, I stepped into the role to understand as best I could the needs of the African American community and then to propose strategies and policies and programs and practices that could improve conditions for African Americans.... The things I had in mind were not consistent with what some — unfortunately, too many — on the board had in mind."

So, it's no surprise that the NAACP would pick a 35 year old, Ben Jealous, to head the organization. You couldn't find a more leftist person than Jealous. But, most importantly, Bond can control him because he doesn't have the stature of a Bruce Gordon.

How can an organization be effective with a 64 member board of directors? It's impossible to make timely decisions with that many people meddling in the day to day operations. Can the general public name anything the organization has accomplished within the past couple of years? It's also noteworthy that few companies on Black Enterprise's top 100 businesses donate any money to the group nor many professional athletes or entertainers.

Why should white America support something that our own people don't support? After 100 years, maybe they have lived 25 years too long. Just something to think about.

Ties That Blind

Published: August 20, 2009

D espite all the problems in the U.S., this is still one of the best places in the world to live. This is why people are committing crimes to enter our country. But, listening to some of the words being used in the healthcare debate, you wouldn't know that.

In last week's column, "The Right Is Wrong," I discussed how people assert their rights, but never assert their responsibilities. Based on the amount of email I received from last week, I must have struck a chord.

Yes, people do have the right to free speech, but they also have the right to leave the country if they are that dissatisfied. Why would you want to live in a country run by a"Nazi?" If Obama's policies are socialist, communist, fascist, what does that make Bush's (and the Republican Congress from then) policies?

You don't hear these people asserting their right to leave the country! Are they so blinded by ideology and racism that they can't distinguish between disagreeing on policy and not accepting the fact that Obama is president?

Can you name another president that has had people show up for a meeting openly displaying guns? Legally, they may have the right, but is it the responsible thing to do?

There is no way to say these acts do not have a racial sub-plot (even though one of the people displaying an assault rifle was Black). This was a great opportunity for the National Rifle Association (NRA) to score some political points by publically calling for restraint and common sense. This has nothing to do with rights and everything to do with being responsible. Folks toting guns at events like these are hurting the NRA brand and it would be wise for their leadership to make some type of public statement. I don't expect them to do this, but it would be a smart move.

Sometimes people can be so blinded by those they choose to associate with. Most of these people have no friends who have differing opinions on various issues, so their whole being is constantly reinforced by those who view the world as they do.

Members of Congress no longer socialize across party lines after votes. Christian conservatives have no interaction with NARAL (abortion rights group). Gay activist has no dialogue with conservative ministers. Any contact with the other is mostly adversarial.

That's why I have made a commitment to having people on my radio show that I totally disagree with on issues (www.ustalknetwork.com). For example, two weeks ago I had John Goodwin from the Humane Society of America on my radio show to talk about the Michael Vick situation. He was a phenomenal guest and he and I are going to get together for lunch or dinner so we can continue our dialogue. Who can know what will come of these friendly conversations.

Just because you disagree doesn't mean you have to be disagreeable. Sometimes we must interact with those with different views so that we can become more understanding of the bigger picture. Even if you don't change your views, at least you have established relationships that will be bigger than individual issues.

So, as people continue to assert their rights, please be cognizant that America is one of the few countries that have this level of freedom. America, with all its blemishes, can be so much better if we focus more on asserting our rights in a more responsible manner.

Associating only with people you agree with is the type of ties that can blind!

A Liberal Solution to Black Unemployment

Published: March 25, 2010

Every time I try to give radical, Black, liberals the benefit of the doubt when it comes to doing what's in the best interest of our own community, I am saddened to conclude that I doubt that there is any benefit.

They claim to represent the Black community, but yet at every turn they undermine the very people they are supposed to be helping. If white people did to us what we are doing to ourselves, there would be a great uproar throughout the country.

The national unemployment rate is 9.7 %, but within the Black community it is 16.5% (12.6% for Hispanics). The Congressional Black Caucus (CBC) has implored the president to create more job training and small business programs for the minority community. Barbara Lee, chairman of the CBC, stated, "This is a deplorable situation.

The facts speak for themselves, and we have to make sure the unemployment rate is addressed throughout the country—and to address the gap. We are saying, for communities of color, we have to look at job training so the gap is closed and look at ways to address systemic unemployment."

The CBC has joined forces with groups like the NAACP and the National Urban League to deal with this issue. Last month, Obama met privately with NAACP president, Ben Jealous, Urban League president, Marc Morial, and Al Sharpton. No one from the CBC was invited. Their absence spoke volumes!

All Blacks should have been insulted that these people were the ones chosen by Obama to talk with him about job creation within the Black community. None of these people or organizations has any knowledge about job creation or economics. This was a cynical political move by the White House to silence the criticism of Obama within the Black community.

So, what is the radical, Black, liberal solution to Black unemployment? They support amnesty for those in the country illegally. These illegals suppress wages and eliminate Blacks from low skilled jobs they would otherwise get. If illegals were removed from the equation, then wages would rise and low skilled people would be better able to support themselves. But, they can't compete with illegals who are willing to work for 70% less than the market rate wage.

So, let me make sure I understand the liberal argument. Black are disproportionally impacted my high unemployment, so they want to inject 20 million more people into the job market by giving amnesty to those who are here illegally, thereby making the high Black unemployment even higher! WOW, ok, now this makes sense. All in the name of building coalitions with the Latino community, we are willing to sacrifice our own people. How can you feed your neighbor, if your own kids haven't eaten? Yes, this is a zero sum game!

Last week, the Washington Post newspaper did a very insightful article about this topic. According to Vernon Briggs, a professor emeritus of industrial and labor relations at Cornell University, "the issue of job competition remains. What we have got here is people using immigration as a political issue to unite certain segments of the population, regardless of the economic and labor market impact. In my view, African American workers are the most adversely affected of all groups, but many legal immigrants in the Hispanic community are also severely impacted because they are disproportionately in the low-skilled labor market where the illegal immigrants compete."

"This new generation of leaders (in the Hispanic community) recognize the need to build stronger coalitions," Morial said. "It is very important that the nation's communities of color do not simply see themselves as groups competing for crumbs."

Jealous, from the NAACP, said "There is a need for a floor for how all workers are treated." There is a need to ensure that nobody in this country can be forced to work in near-slavery-like conditions. So much of the black experience has been about us fighting over centuries to be part of this country, and for Latinos it's a similar story."

Are these guys crazy? They accuse Obama of not doing enough about Black unemployment, but yet they want to increase the number of people competing for a finite number of low skilled jobs? In the immortal words of George W. Bush, "this is fuzzy math."

I could at least understand this cooperation if they had the good sense to extract some type of concession from the Latino community. For example, why won't the Latino community speak out on the racist policy that allows Cubans (mostly white Cubans) to stay in the country based on the idiotic "wet foot, dry foot policy?" Simply put, the policy states that if a Cuban gets one foot on U.S. soil, then they are granted the chance to remain in the country and later would qualify for expedited legal permanent resident status and U.S. citizenship. Contrast that with people from Haiti who are summarily returned immediately to their country with no hope of getting an opportunity for citizenship.

How long will these so called Black leaders continue to sell out their own people and get nothing in return? Blacks must think strategically, not emotionally. It is totally idiotic to support a policy that will hurt the very people you claim to represent. I can no longer give these radical, Black, liberal individuals the benefit of the doubt because I doubt that there is any benefit.

Alienation

Published: April 29, 2010

My position on illegal immigration is very public—I DO NOT SUPPORT AMNESTY under any circumstances. So, with the new illegal immigration bill signed into law in Arizona and the volume of phone calls seeking my opinion, I have decided to share my thoughts on this issue.

But this time, I want to try a different approach. Those who are interested in my detailed views on illegal immigration can go to my website and read some of my previous columns of this subject. In this column, I will pose a series of questions and make some observations that will, hopefully stimulate a more reasoned debate on this issue.

As written in previous columns, how can the NAACP (supposedly the premier civil rights organization in the

U.S.) support amnesty for over 30 million people and yet complain to Obama about the high unemployment rate in the Black community? So, their solution is to increase the pool of unskilled workers who will compete with citizens of this country for a limited number of unskilled jobs!

Why is Al Sharpton sticking his nose into the business of Arizona? He is threatening to organize boycotts, yada, yada, yada! I wish he would devote the same level of energy to the racist "wet foot, dry foot" policy that is in effect in Miami, Florida. This insane policy allows any Cuban who gets at least one foot on U.S. shore to stay, but if a Haitian does the same thing, he is immediately returned to his country. Where is Al Sharpton on this issue? Oh, I forgot, there is no camera crew there to cover this story.

If we can strip away all the emotion on both sides, I think it will become very clear why Americans are not in a mood to forgive criminals for coming into our country and be told what their rights are. Let's establish the fact that they broke the law—regardless of their reasons, they are lawbreakers! If I rob someone because I have no money to feed my family, I have still violated the law and deserve to be punished. My having a good reason is not enough to absolve me of the crime committed.

Please, my amnesty supporters, tell me why an illegal (they are NOT undocumented, they are **ILLEGAL**) person should get in-state tuition for college, but a U.S. citizen can't get the same benefit? Why should illegals be able to get free health care and there is none for U.S. citizens? Americans receive more immigrants annually than the sum total of all other countries combined. We are very much pro-immigration, not illegal immigration.

My pro amnesty friends want us to forgive illegals, but these same people won't spend the same energy restoring voting rights to felons who have been released from prison. They have paid their dues to society, but still carry the brand of being a felon. Are you kidding me? You want me to get upset over how we treat those who broke into our country, but overlook those who served their time and still can't get a break? In the immortal words of Chad "Ocho Cinco" Johnson, "Child please!"

When I go to foreign countries, if I don't speak the language, then I am out of luck. But, yet California prints their election ballots in over 200 languages. We are enabling foreigners not to assimilate. If you are or want to be an American, then you must speak English.

I guarantee that none of my pro amnesty friends know who Robert Krentz was. Well, he was the Arizona rancher that was murdered by an illegal a couple weeks ago. He is the reason the bill in Arizona was passed. But his death has been lost in all the emotion of the debate. No one is talking about the impact that illegals who are committing crimes are having on U.S. families.

When will we focus on the rights of Americans to be safe more than the non-existent rights of those who are illegal? Rights are earned with responsible behavior. Would someone please tell me what are the responsibilities that illegals have to America? You never hear illegals talking about their responsibilities, only what their rights are.

This attitude is what is grating on Americans. The only right illegals have is the right to leave the country. Obama has the right, er, obligation to enforce the existing laws of the land. If we don't step up enforcement of existing laws and punish employers that hire illegals, then Obama and the Democrats will only continue to fuel this alienation!

The "Am Nasty" Debate

Published: May 20, 2010

I am really getting fed up with my liberal friends saying that because I am against amnesty for illegals, I am nasty! Unfortunately, our society has devolved into a mindset where if you disagree with someone, you must have bad motives.

The pro-amnesty crowd is up in arms over the recently passed Arizona bill that takes a very tough line on illegals. Their contention is that it will lead to racial profiling. I challenge anyone with a brain to actually read the law and come to that conclusion. But, they assert that if a person is "legitimately" stopped my law enforcement and is then found to be illegal, they would not have an issue with the person being brought before an immigration court.

Of course, these are just idle words. Liberals don't really believe that. They want blanket amnesty for every illegal in the country, PERIOD!

There is an interesting court case percolating through the courts in Cobb County, Georgia (a suburb of Atlanta). I won't go into all the details, but you can read the full

account at:
http://www.nytimes.com/2010/05/15/us/15student.html?hpw.

On March 29, 2010, Jessica Colotl, a 21 year-old illegal Mexican college student at Kennesaw State University, was pulled over by a campus policeman for "impeding the flow of traffic." She had no valid driver's license, but instead presented an expired Mexican passport. She was immediately arrested and sent to the county jail where she admitted that she was in the country illegally. Two weeks ago the sheriff filed a felony charge against her for providing a false address to the police.

On May 5, she was transferred to the Etowah Detention Center in Alabama to await deportation to Mexico. But, after loud protests from pro-amnesty groups and a letter of support from the president of the university, Immigration and Customs Enforcement (ICE) granted her a one year deferral on her deportation in order to finish college (she is 1 year away from graduation).

Now call me crazy, but what does her graduation have to do with her breaking the laws of the U.S.? So, if she was illegal and busted for selling drugs, would she be allowed to finish school before her case was adjudicated? Either we are going to enforce the law or we are not. So, the next time an American citizen is accused of a crime, I hope the judge will let them out on a $ 2,500 bond so they can finish school!

This is the very issue that the pro-amnesty crowd doesn't get—illegals seem to get rights and privileges that not even citizens are able to get. Oh, did I tell you that she was getting instate tuition? But the student from Alabama had to pay out of state tuition, which costs about twice as much as what the illegal had to pay. Ms. Colotl was so cocky after being released on bond that she decided to hold her own press conference. You talk about ARROGANCE! According to her, "I never thought that I'd be caught up in this messed-up system....I was treated like a criminal, like a threat to the nation." Well, duh, you are a criminal. You broke our laws and then have the nerve to criticize our system? Then go back to your country.

Her pro-amnesty supporters say that Colotl should not be deported because she was brought her by her parents when she was 11 (thus, it's pretty clear that her parents are in the country illegally also). Their argument is that she is excelling in school and was discovered to be here illegally only after a routine traffic violation.

Now, I am totally confused. The pro-amnesty crowd opposes the Arizona law because of the fear of being racially profiled. Now, in Georgia, the police did everything by the book and they still don't want to have an illegal deported. So, it is quite obvious that the Arizona law is not the real issue. These folks will settle for nothing short of total amnesty, with no conditions.

No one disputes that Colotl violated state law (traffic) and lied to the police about her address (a felony). And their strongest argument is that she has one year left for completion of college? Mexico has plenty of universities!

Mary Bauer, according to the New York Times article, the legal director for the Southern Poverty Law Center, which is assisting in Ms. Colotl's defense, said Cobb County had a history of using federal laws designed to detect dangerous criminals for arresting illegal immigrants for minor offenses. "This is a civil rights disaster," said Ms. Bauer, who called the county's application of the law "mean-spirited and very probably illegal."

Oh, I see, so the application of the law should be based on the severity of the crime, not based on the written statute. Either Colotl broke the law or she didn't; either she is here legally or illegally. You can't have laws based on feelings ("mean-spirited"). This is why Americans have strong feelings about not granting amnesty to illegals. This debate has nothing to do with whether I am nasty, but rather me being against amnesty.

Amnesty is a "Terror-ble" Idea

Published: June 3, 2010

A m I the only who is sick and tired of illegals telling me what their rights are in this country? Am I the only one who is sick and tired of pro-amnesty groups trotting out all the sob stories from illegals—"their mother brought them here when they were little kids, etc.?" It's not about rights; it's about what is right!

Is it right for illegals to get free healthcare when citizens do not? Is it right for illegals to get in-state tuition for university when citizens do not?

Amnesty for illegals is a terrible idea if for no other reason than the right of citizens to be safe. Our intelligence community has known for decades that terrorists have infiltrated our country by crossing the border from Mexico. Americans have a right to be safe in their own country. So, for once, let's talk about the rights of U.S. citizens over the "nonexistent" rights of illegals!

According to an Associated Press (AP) story last week, "the Department of Homeland Security warned Houston law enforcement that a Somali terrorist named Mohamed Ali could be in their area. Ali is a member of al-Shabaab, the terrorist group currently fighting for control of Somalia. Al-Shabaab has proven to be frighteningly effective at recruiting Westerners, including Americans." The point of entry for Ali was through Mexico. I find it quite interesting that the alert was never released to the public, but was leaked to media outlets. This government doesn't want you to know the seriousness of the border problems.

Let's assume for the sake of discussion that amnesty was granted. Illegals in the U.S. from various countries come forward to register with the government. If Jose Santaballo or Mohammed Akbar presents themselves as coming from Mexico and Somalia, respectively; how do we know if they are who they say they are? What vehicle will we use to prove these are their birth names and how can we prove they were not criminals or terrorists in their home country?

More than likely, they created a whole new identity with fake documents when they entered the U.S. illegally. For those who came in legally and overstayed their visa, how do we do a retroactive background check? Or do we just let everyone self-certify that they are good people?

Illegal immigration is not about the rights of illegals, it's about the rights of American citizens to be safe and to know who is in our country. So, enough of the boring sob stories about the illegals; no more discussing their rights; and please, no more lecturing from foreigners about our immigration laws.

Americans were insulted two weeks ago by Mexican president, Felipe Calderon, last week by a Somali diplomat, Omar Jamal (first secretary of the Somali mission at the United Nations), and this week by Peruvian president, Alan Garcia.

Calderon called Arizona's recently passed illegal immigration law "discriminatory" and said it would lead to "racial profiling." But he failed to mention that Mexico's own immigration laws are a lot more stringent than Arizona's or our federal law (and unlike the U.S., they enforce their immigration laws). Jamal, of Somalia, has the gall to talk about law and order when he is from a country that has no laws! Garcia called the Arizona law a "completely irrational response" to illegal-immigration. Like Peru is the citadel of human rights!

Am I the only one who is sick and tired of America becoming the international punching bag of choice because, we the people, demand to know who is in our country? This is not just about Obama; this is about

Obama, our president. I have never seen a U.S. president insulted (and by extension the American people) on our soil so continuously and yet seems to accept it. America is becoming the laughing stock of the world.

This has ominous foreign policy implications. Say what you will about George W. Bush, but he would not have allowed this to happen. Many countries hated Bush, but they never challenged our might. It is far better to be feared than it is to be loved when it comes to foreign affairs.

If our laws and our country is so discriminatory, if we need lectures on law and order, or if our laws are "completely irrational;" then why is everyone trying to get into America and not the countries that are lecturing us?

Therefore, giving amnesty to illegals is not only a terrible idea; it is extremely dangerous when you don't know who is in your country. Before the year is out, there will be a terrorist attack on our soil and the perpetrator (s) will be traced back through the Mexican border. Then and only then will we get serious about securing our border. Then, the thought of giving amnesty to illegals will not only be a terrible idea, but a terror-ble thought.

Only in Black America

Published: February 17, 2011

Last year I wrote a column about how President Obama totally disrespected Black America (during Black History Month of all times) and there was no outcry from within our community.

Now, you have the same thing happening again, of course during Black History Month. This time the offender is the illustrious Washington Post (WP) newspaper. They are supposed to be one of the top newspapers in the country, so this makes their offense even more egregious.

Next Wednesday, the WP will be hosting a town hall meeting in Prince Georges County, Maryland. For those who live outside of this area, this is the wealthiest Black county in America.

This is how the Washington Post is advertising the event: "Please join The Washington Post for an informative panel discussion, **"Behind the Headlines: A Discussion on Race and the Recession in Metro Washington."** The panel will cover the recession's impact on local black families and will look at how economic policies in Washington have affected African Americans. The forum will also look at the first of three groundbreaking public opinion polls on issues facing the black community, conducted by The Washington Post, the Kaiser Family Foundation and Harvard University.

Washington Post nationally syndicated personal finance columnist **Michelle Singletary** will moderate the discussion, and panelists will include **Julianne Malveaux**, a noted economist and educator; **Cecilia Rouse**, a member of the White House Council of Economic Advisers; **Rep. Emanuel Cleaver**, chairman of the Congressional Black Caucus; **Michael A. Fletcher**, a Washington Post national economics reporter; the **Rev. Al Sharpton**, president of the National Action Network; and **Jeff Johnson**, a political commentator on the nationally syndicated "Tom Joyner Morning Show."

So, you might ask, what is the issue I have with the WP? Just as I questioned President Obama's choice of people to meet with him in the White House last year about the high unemployment rate within the Black community, I have the same thoughts about the WP.

The moderator of the panel is a journalist, followed by a radical leftist economist, another liberal economist, a

preacher/politician, a journalist, another preacher/politician, and finally, a political commentator. You have got to be joking!
Prince Georges County is home to some of the most successful Black businessmen in the U.S. and not one has been invited to participate. Five of the seven panelists are known Democrats (with Singletary and Fletcher having no known public political affiliation).

Is there any particular reason why the WP conveniently decided not to have any Black Republicans on the panel? Of course it could not be because they are biased. The Post would never travel down that path, would they? Of course they would and they have!

For all practical purposes, this will be an unpaid political commercial for the Obama reelection campaign. The panelists (with the exception of 2) all are in agreement with most of Obama's approach to the economy. So, how can you have a serious discussion with people who already agree with each other?

It should not be surprising that 5 of the 7 panelists have ties to the Obama administration (formal or informal). One of the constant criticisms of President Obama is that he has no one around him from the private sector.

None of these panelists have ever created a job, so what is it that they have to say that is relevant?

The last thing the Black community needs is another theoretical discussion. Even socialism works in a 'theoretical' world. I can tell you everything that will be said next week and I won't even be there.

At what point are Blacks going to rise up against this insulting pandering? With all the super successful people in this town, the WP couldn't find any businessmen to talk about these issues? Why did they not invite any educators, like the dean of Howard University's Business school, Dr. Barron Harvey?

After this event, then what? Blacks will go there to hear all the usual arguments: racism, Republican budget cuts, Bush created the problems, etc.

So, I challenge the Washington Post to underwrite a town hall meeting that I will put together to deal with these issues in a more serious manner. I will moderate the panel and assemble a group of panelist who will offer real world solutions to these problems.

I don't expect the Post to respond to my challenge; for to do so would be admitting they made a huge mistake.

In the immortal words of the Godfather of Soul, James Brown, "like a dull knife—just ain't cutting it; you just talking loud and saying nothing."

The Media's Foreign Policy

Published: February 24, 2011

The media in general and the American media in particular continue to bring shame to what's left of the profession once called journalism. They have long ago conceded the principles of objectivity and reporting strictly "the facts." They seem more interested in becoming a celebrity or injecting themselves into the story, rather than reporting the story.

The media does a grave injustice to their profession by attempting to give overly simplistic coverage to what are extremely complicated foreign policy issues.

The upheaval that is going on in Tunisia, Egypt, Libya, etc., has nothing to do with democracy. For the media to report such is totally irresponsible. Such reporting presupposes a universal definition of the meaning of democracy.

The people of Iraq voted for a theocracy. Can a theocracy be a democracy? What happens if the people of Egypt vote in a member of the Muslim Brotherhood as president? Is that a democracy?

The American media never goes deeper into the complexity of international issues. This is one of the major reasons why Americans, especially students, rank at the bottom of most things dealing with international issues.

American journalists stupidly called the uprising in Tunisia the Facebook revolution. It had absolutely nothing to do with Facebook or any other single thing; it was a combination of things all happening simultaneously.

If there was one single factor that could have been the trigger that set all this in motion, it would have to be age. Some refer to this as the "youth bulge." The average age in Tunisia is 29 and in Egypt, 24. But, yet the age of their two former leaders were 74 and 82 respectively.

The populations in these countries are very literate and very tech savvy. Most of these people have never seen a typewriter or a land line telephone; but they might have satellite TV at home and a mobile phone with internet connection. They are global citizens, though they have never left their own soil.

The thirst for freedom, not democracy (whatever that means), is the driving force behind this unrest. The older population has accepted their lives as it is—that's all they know. But, the youth have envisioned that better life and nothing will stop them from getting it.

What is transpiring in Northern Africa and the Middle East, will be visiting sub-Saharan Africa by the fall. Before cell phones and the internet, people in developing countries could only read about the American dream. But, now, through technology, they can see, hear, and live it in real time.

Technology is the water that nourished the seeds that were planted in these people from childhood. Go to school, go to university, they were told and your country will give you a better life. Well, millions have done this, only to find their dreams turning into a nightmare. They can't find a job in their own country. They can't get a visa to go to the U.S. or the U.K. So, when you go to a developing country and eat at the hotel restaurant; don't be surprised that the person that is serving you has a master's degree in business or engineering.

They have lost hope, so there is no fear of death. They have nothing to lose, so they take to the street with the thinking that it can only get better. The blood of a few, is the seed corn for the liberation of the many.

Sub-Saharan African has a population of over 800 million people, with over half being under 18 years of age. This is a huge growth market for our future exports. This is why we tolerate despots around the world. We will tolerate Obiang in Equatorial Guinea (because of their oil), Mubarak in Egypt (he was a critical ally in the war on terror), etc.

I would argue that over the next 25 years, sub-Saharan African is going to be more vital to the U.S.'s national security than either China, India, Saudi Arabia, or even Israel.

But, the media tries to cover these complicated stories in sound bites, even on their websites. Part of the responsibility of a journalist is to educate their audience. For their profession not to do so, I find a foreign policy.

The Root Of The Problem Is "The Root"

Published: March 3, 2011

I n agriculture, if the root of the plant goes bad, so goes the rest of the plant. Above the ground, the plant may be very beautiful, but internally it is dying.

This reminds me of "The Root" online magazine. According to their website: "The Root is a daily online magazine that provides thought-provoking commentary on today's news from a variety of black perspectives." They are owned and published by the Washington Post Newsweek Interactive.

The Root was launched on January 28th, 2008. According to media accounts, "The Root" was created by Donald Graham, Chairman of The Washington Post Company and Henry Louis Gates Jr., the Alphonse Fletcher University Professor at Harvard and Director of the W.E.B. Du Bois Institute for African and African American Research. Gates went on to say, "it will feature penetrating, lively commentary on political, social and cultural issues, and will showcase the breadth and depth of viewpoints currently shaping black culture."

Lynette Clemetson, one of the original editors, was quoted in several newspaper articles, "The Root' resists the notion that there is--or ever was--such a thing as a monolithic black community. The Web site will be a forum for true conversation, celebrating the rich mix of voices, issues and points of view that bring nuance and complexity to the black experience. And while the site is committed to topics of special interest to blacks, it is a destination for anyone interested in the dynamic link between history and our collective future."

Oh, really? Would to God that Gates and Clemetson really meant what they said above. "The Root" was founded by liberals/Democrats (Donald Graham and the Washington Post are well known for their very liberal slant; and Gates comes from the same mold.). Neither the founding management nor the current management has any known conservatives/Republicans in its employ.

"The Root" has done the same thing that Blacks have so often accused whites of doing—putting all liberals in management, but printing a few editorials from conservative/Republicans who are Black. Then they say, "see, we have diversity!"

But everyone in news knows that the power lies with the editors (executive, managing, assignment), not with the writers. These editors not only decide what subjects are written about, but also, how the final story is presented to the public. So, if the management all comes from the same bias, where is the diversity of thought and opinion?

So Mr. Gates states, "it [The Root] will feature penetrating, lively commentary on political, social and cultural issues, and will showcase the breadth and depth of viewpoints currently shaping black culture." Is this what he had in mind when he and management created a section with the title, "The Blackest White Folks We Know" (http://www.theroot.com/multimedia/blackest-white-folks-we-know)? Are you kidding me? Is this Gates' definition of "penetrating'? I am thoroughly embarrassed that an esteemed academic like Gates would perpetuate the foolishness that we have accused whites of doing. What next? The "Whitest Black Man?"

According to Ms. Clemetson, "The Root' resists the notion that there is--or ever was--such a thing as a monolithic black community." Is this what management had in mind when they created a section with the title, "The Black Folks We'd Remove From Black History?" (http://www.theroot.com/multimedia/black-folks-wed-remove-black-history). Who is the "we?" Who decided who would be on the list and who wouldn't? I find their comments about Supreme Court Justice Clarence Thomas reprehensible.

The most painful thing is that these two sections are in the top three sections visited on the site. Am I the only one that is embarrassed by this section of the site? Am I the only one who is willing to publically criticize management for this hypocrisy?

Remember, these sections are not in the opinion section. This content is solely that of management. It is quite obvious that management is very liberal in its bias.

How can we, in the Black community, complain about how others portray us and then we do the same thing we have accused them of doing—namely, using the basest of all stereotypes, stymie content that management disagrees with, and have absolutely no diversity within management. Shouldn't Jesse Jackson and Al Sharpton demand diversity from the Washington Post? When will they begin the picketing?

The site looks good, it's very appealing to the eye, and does have some very good articles and commentary. But, like dying vegetation, when you begin to look at the roots, you find "The Root" is the problem.

Feminism Lays An Egg

Published: March 10, 2011

When you ask a chicken for an egg, it's like asking for a contribution. Chickens lay many, many eggs in the course of their lifetime. But, when you ask a pig for bacon, you're asking for a total commitment. In other words, the pig has to die in order to give you that bacon.

This should be the essence of having children, especially from the woman's perspective. When you decide to have children, your life stops because your raison d'être is to provide for that child—mentally, physically, spiritually, and emotionally. You are no longer being asked for an egg, you are being asked to give bacon.

But, the pursuit of the feminist agenda has turned this view upside down. Many women believe they can have it all—marriage, children, and career. This is the core of the feminist agenda. Last month, we had a very perverse example of the feminist agenda on steroids.

Amber Branson is a 34 year old girl's high school basketball coach in Lipan, TX (about 75 miles from Dallas). She was pregnant and expected to deliver her child at any moment.

Her basketball team had a semi-final game in Abilene and she decided to make the trip with the team. After winning the game, she went back to her hotel and began to have labor pains. She was taken to the hospital (this was on a Friday night) and delivered her child just after 10 p.m.

Her team had another game, the finals, the next day (Saturday) at 2 p.m. Yep, you guessed it. She left the hospital and her newborn to coach the team. Yes, you heard right! She left a newborn in the care of total strangers. In an interview after the game (her team won and went on to lose in the championship game) she said, "I didn't do anything that didn't feel like I was supposed to be doing. And I just wanted to be with the girls...I don't think it's anything special...But it's just part of my job and I was just happy to be a part of it." In another interview she said, "That was all part of God's plan. If I had the epidural, I might not have been able to make [the game]...I would have taken [newborn daughter Leslie] with me if I could have."

Has she lost her mind? Leaving a newborn, not because of some family emergency, but to coach a basketball game! I don't know of any sane woman who would have done something this irresponsible. Social services should definitely take custody of the child. Branson, is quite obviously not fit to be a parent, even though she has two other children.

I am just as stunned that the husband seems to be OK with this bizarre behavior. Guess we know who wears the pants in this family!

With this type of irrational behavior, we should not be surprised that she then turns around and blames God ("that was all a part of God's plan"). God had absolutely nothing to do with this.

What kind of example is she setting for the girls on her team, as well as her own children? Just think, in the first day of her child's life, she spent almost the same amount of time with the girls on her basketball team as she did with her own baby!

If her job is that important to her, then she should not have children. Ms. Branson, YOU CAN'T HAVE IT ALL! With every choice there is a consequence. You choose a basketball game at the expense of your daughter. What a sad commentary on the state of femininity.

To my amazement, I haven't heard any of the usual feminist groups denounce this irresponsible behavior, especially the National Organization of Women (NOW). Branson is not fit to be a parent, nor continue to coach her team.   She has proven she is not capable of making responsible decisions with her own family, so how can you justify entrusting other kids to her care?

When it comes to parenting, Branson laid an egg, as opposed to providing bacon to her newborn daughter. Her daughter needed a total commitment, not a contribution.

Un-"Common" Thoughts

Published: May 12, 2011

L ast night Michelle Obama hosted an "Evening of Poetry" at the White House. She invited an eclectic group of poets to recite their poetry. But, Fox News and right wing radio has singled out one performer—the Grammy award winning rapper Common—to be on the receiving end of their ire.

I don't listen to his music, but from talking with friends who know him, he seems to be a nice enough guy and is very talented! But, he has one song about shooting a policeman, therefore conservative media objected to him being invited to the White House.

These conservatives are now making the argument, that since Common was invited to the White House, President and Ms. Obama must agree with his lyrics. Anyone with a brain knows this is idiotic, but welcome to the world of right wing media.

The Obama's have a right to invite whomever they choose to the White House.

You can't take a single or few events in a person's life and let that be the definitive narrative of his life. For example, Michael Vick should not have his whole life defined by his run in with the law if he continues to exemplify the level of maturity he has in the past year. We all make mistakes.

Common, born Lonnie Rashid Lynn, Jr., hails from Chicago, IL. He had a middle class upbringing and attended Florida A & M University where he studied business. He has earned two Grammys (best R & B song in 2003 for "Love of My Life and best rap performance by a duo or group in 2007 for "Southside").

Though an unabashed liberal, he has dedicated himself to trying to make a positive difference in the lives of the youth. For this, he should be commended!

What I find amazing about right wing media is they seem to be for free speech—as long as they agree with what you are saying.

If they were consistent with their feigned outrage over Common, then I could accept their views. But, I find their outrage very inconsistent and very selective. They make it seem as though Obama is the only president to associate with an entertainer who have expressed some controversial things.

Where was their outrage over former president Ronald Reagan's tribute to Bruce Springsteen?

On September 19, 1984, Reagan was at a campaign stop in Hammonton, New Jersey and he said, "America's future rests in a thousand dreams inside your hearts…it rests in the message of hope in songs so many young Americans admire…New Jersey's own Bruce Springsteen." Springsteen is best known for his monster hit song "Born in the U.S.A." But, on this same album is a song titled "Working On The Highway." The song is about a man who has sex with an underage girl and is subsequently arrested by the police and convicted in a court of law. Here are a few of the words:

"I saved up my money and I put it all away
I went to see her daddy but we didn't have much to say
"Son can't you see that she's just a little girl
She don't know nothing about this cruel cruel world"

We lit out down to Florida we got along all right
One day her brothers came and got her and they took me in a black and white (*police car*)
The prosecutor kept the promise that he made on that day
And the judge got mad and he put me straight away

I wake up every morning to the work bell clang (*jail*)
Me and the warden go swinging on the Charlotte County
road gang
Working on the highway...

President Nixon invited racist Elvis Presley to the White House. Presley spent a lifetime letting people know how he felt about Blacks!

President Carter invited the legendary group, Crosby, Stills, & Nash to visit him in the White House. According to their own biography, "One of us, and I will not say who, lit a joint in the Oval Office just to be able to say he'd done it, you know?"

The other irony is that a lot of these same conservatives claim very publically their friendship to entertainers whose lyrics are no different than those they criticize Common for.

Sarah Palin is a huge fan of rocker, Ted Nugent. Here are the words to one of his songs, "Wang Dang Sweet Poontang."

That Nadine, what a teenage queen...She lookin' so clean, especi'lly down in between...She's so sweet when she yanks on my meat." Is this the type of "family values" Palin has in mind?

Last year Elton John was reportedly paid $1 million to perform at Rush Limbaugh's wedding reception. John is the same person who referred to Christians as "Jesus Freaks" in his hit song "Tiny Dancer."

When right wing media begin to show their moral outrage evenly, then and only then, can I support their feigned righteous indignation. But, until then, they should remain quiet and focus on the more pressing issues facing our country.

They should also show some respect for the office of the president. This should be a common courtesy!

Black Women No Longer Have Their Essence

Published: May 26, 2011

Essence Magazine used to be the preeminent magazine for Black women in the U.S. They, like many Black publications, have lost their relevance; and in the process become an embarrassment to the very group they claim to target.

Essence was founded in 1968 by Ed Lewis, Clarence Smith, Cecil Hollingworth, Jonathan Blount, and Denise Clark. Their initial circulation began at around 50,000 per month and now is estimated to be over 1 million per month. It is a monthly publication focusing on Black women between the ages of 18 and 49. Essence was bought out by Time Inc. in 2005, thus no longer being a Black owned publication (similar to B.E.T.).

The impetus behind the founding of Essence was to show a side of Black women that was never portrayed in the mainstream media. Images of Black women were controlled by white media outlets that had little to no knowledge of the Black community. Most of these images were very stereotypical and lacking substance.

There were unique issues relevant to Black women that other publications were totally ignorant of. Black women could not wear the same makeup that white women could---there are differences in skin type. Black women have unique issues when it comes to styling their hair—there were no mainstream publications that dealt with these differences.

So, initially, Essence met a very real need and provided a venue for Black women to share common experiences with each other (remember, this was pre-internet days when you didn't have all the instant communication we have today).

Essence portrayed Black women in the most positive of lights. They made Black women feel proud to be Black and female! That was then, this is now.

Now, Essence is just another Hollywood rag (focused on Black women), sprinkled with a few substantive, positive stories; but, that is no longer their focus!

I looked at the cover picture for the past year and each cover featured an entertainer. Isn't this the same stereotyping that we have accused white media of—showing Blacks as only entertainers? There is nothing wrong with having entertainers on the cover, but is that all there is to offer Black women?

I can guarantee that most Black women have never heard of Sadie Tanner Mossell Alexander, Alicia Jillian Hardy, or Katie Washington.

When I went on Essence Music Festival's website and looked at the speakers listed under "Empowerment." I was stunned and quite embarrassed!

The Essence Music Festival is the nation's largest annual gathering of Black musical talent in the U.S. It is a 3 day event filled with cultural celebrations, empowerment panels, and nightly entertainment by some of the biggest names in music. It is held in New Orleans, LA every July. The event attracts more than 200,000 people.

One of the speakers listed under "Empowerment" is "NeNe" Leakes. She is one of the main characters of the reality TV show, "The Real Housewives of Atlanta. The show is about the private lives of women who are dating or is married to successful men in the Atlanta area.

Leakes is a foul mouth, angry, nasty person on the show and from media accounts in real life also. She is also the founder of Twisted Hearts Foundation (which focuses on domestic violence against women). They were forced to close down last year after being suspected of money laundering. Leakes is also a former stripper.

One of the other speakers listed under "Empowerment" is Shaunie O'Neal, former wife of N.B.A. great Shaquille O'Neal. She is the executive producer of "Basketball Wives." The women's only claim to fame is that they either dated or were married to a pro basketball player. They have no identity outside the athletes they were involved with.

Both shows portray women in the worst light imaginable—using high profile men to get fame and fortune. These women then try to exploit their former relationships to get their own TV show. They are paid to tell the most intimate details of their former relationships.

Essence, could you please tell me how these two women fit into your mission of uplifting the Black woman? What can they teach women about "empowerment?" Is this really the image of Black women Essence wants to promote? There are many women who could fit into your mission statement.

By the way, Sadie Tanner Mossell Alexander was the first Black woman to earn a Ph.D. in America (1921). Alicia Jillian Hardy is the first Black woman to earn a Ph.D from M.I.T. in mechanical engineering (2007). Katie Washington, a 21 year old, became the first Black female valedictorian in the history of Notre Dame University

(2010). She gave a wonderful speech (http://www.youtube.com/watch?v=VaouUZrn2vI).

One would think that Ms. Hardy and Washington deserved to be on the cover for their achievements; and most assuredly know a little something about empowerment! Oh, I forgot, they are not entertainers, so they don't qualify.

In times past, Black women used to look forward to reading Essence Magazine for upliftment. That was then, this is now. Black women no longer have the Essence of their mother and grandmother.

In Essence, there is no essence!

The Real HU

Published: October 6, 2011

Howard University, in Washington, D.C., is one of the elite Historically Black Colleges and Universities (HBCU) in the U.S. Howard students are quick to call their school the "real HU!" The reason is so they won't be confused with another well-known HBCU—Hampton University.

But after years of frustrating experiences with Howard University, I have come to the conclusion that they are truly the "real HU." But, in this case, the HU stands for **"Horrible University."**

Over the years, I have regularly presented Howard and its student's opportunities to make money and to further the mission of their school—to educate Black students.

Last week, I was called by a friend and asked to find 2 law students she could interview for internships in her government agency. I told her I would call Howard's law school and have them call her. I talked with a woman in their career placement office and she said she would call my friend. A week later and my friend still has not heard from the school.

So, 2 days ago, I decided to call George Washington University's Law School (GW)—a predominantly white school in Washington, DC. I told them I needed two Black law students to consider for internships. Less than an hour later, my friend was contacted by GW and 2 lucky students are on the verge of getting an internship!

If my negative experience with Howard was an isolated incident, then I could shrug it off to a thing called life—sometimes things happen. But, this is not the case.

Earlier this year, I called the president of Howard University and offered the school a chance to be the venue for a series of Republican presidential candidate's town hall forums. I am still waiting for them to give me an answer.

Several years ago, a friend of mine who owned all the Domino's Pizzas in this area, offered to give the school a free franchise that the students could run. The only stipulation was that the school donates the space. According to our calculations, each student would have earned about $ 10,000 per year. I have yet to get a response from the school, almost 10 years later!

So, yes Howard, you are the "real HU--" horrible university! So, Howard, you win. I will not attempt to provide any further opportunities to the school, nor its students.

Howard University has a storied past, but not such a storied present. Howard has got to be the worst run HBCU in the country. I had this conversation with a current student at Howard yesterday at a restaurant and she agreed with me 100%.

To Howard and its students, why can I never seem to get a simple response when I try to present opportunities to you? Even if you are not interested, a definitive response would have been appreciated. But that seems too much to ask. Yet, white institutions seem to respond immediately to any offer I present to them.

God has blessed me in many ways, so my only obligation is to reach out my hand, not attempt to make someone take my hand.

In the immortal words of Sir Winston Churchill, "To everyman (or organization) there comes a time when he is figuratively tapped on the shoulder and offered the chance to do a great and might work; unique to him and fitted to his talents; what a tragedy if that moment finds him unprepared or unqualified for the moment that could be his finest hour." Unfortunately, Howard University has been found both unprepared and unqualified!

President Obama: Please Call Home

Published: February 13, 2013

J ust imagine someone in your family travelling half way across the country to help a family they don't know nor have any connection to; while at the same time his own family is in crisis. Just imagine how you would feel if your family barely had food to eat, but yet your father goes across town and gives some of your food to a family that he doesn't even know.

I am sure in both cases the family would feel betrayed and a bit confused; and outsiders would surely think the father has lost his mind. Is it a noble gesture to try to help your fellow man? Of course it is. But, while it might be tragic for another family to be suffering, a father's first obligation is to his own family, then his own community, and then the world.

President Obama, in many ways, serves as our nation's symbolic "father." In times of crisis, we look to him for comfort, support, and direction. Remember Reagan after the Space Shuttle Challenger exploded; Bush 41 after the Rodney King riots; or Bush 43 after 911?

Having worked around 3 presidents, I am fully aware that a president can't be everywhere, all the time and he has to pick and choose how he leads a country in a time of crisis. What a tragedy if that moment finds him unprepared or unqualified for the moment that could be his finest hour.

I found the anemic response by this White House and this president to the senseless death of Hadiya Pendleton very tragic.

Pendleton was a 15 year-old honors student who was shot and killed last Tuesday in Chicago. She had recently performed at President Obama's January 21st inauguration with her high school's band and drill team. She was shot in the back at a neighborhood park. She had just finished taking her exams at King College Prep. According to police, a gunman jumped a fence, ran toward the group of girls and opened fire, then jumped in a car and left the scene. The girls were standing under a canopy to hide themselves from the rain. Pendleton was hit in the back; a male victim, 16, is in serious condition. The park is about 1 mile from Obama's Chicago home.

The White House's response was weak at best and callous at worst. When asked about Pendleton's death, presidential spokesman Jay Carney called it a 'terrible tragedy for someone to be killed when they had so much of their life ahead of them. The president and first lady's thoughts and prayers are with the family of Hadiya Pendleton. All of our thoughts and prayers are with her family.' When Obama was asked about Pendleton's murder, he went into this bizarre rant about, "well, the problem is that a huge proportion of those guns come in from outside Chicago... creating a bunch of pockets of gun laws without a unified, integrated system of background checks makes it harder for a single community to protect itself from gun violence." His response was very creepy, as though he was just a robot, with no connection with his own humanity.

Now juxtapose that with his response to the shootings in Newtown, CT. He shed tears for those kids and takes a trip there, but for Pendleton and others who have been killed this year---just a few terse words.

This year alone, Chicago has had over 42 murders and had 506 total during 2012. Remember, most of these murders occurred within blocks of Obama's Chicago home, surrounded by a full complement of Secret Service agents.

He is driven through these neighborhoods with his military-style entourage, but somehow never finds the time to stop by and talk with some of the families of those who have been murdered, many under the age of 10 years old.

All lives are precious, but I am having a hard time watching my president fly to Newtown, CT., which is a 1,000 miles from Chicago; but, yet he can't walk a couple blocks from his house in Chicago.

I won't apologize for thinking that maybe it has something to do with the zip code of the two cities or the polar opposite economic levels between the two cities. You always try to give a sitting president the benefit of the doubt, but in Obama's case, I doubt if there is any benefit.

Maybe he doesn't view Chicago as part of his family, but rather believes he has more in common with those in Newtown. Just food for thought.

The Destruction of the Black Family

Published: May 16, 2013

I have travelled all over the world and have spent many years of my life studying the history of the world and can't recall any instance of a surviving civilization without an intact family structure—mother, father, and children.

I fully understand that the march towards modernity waits for no one. In communications, we went from teletype to telephones; from newspapers to radio; from radio to TV; from TV to mobile devices.

In transportation, we went from walking to horses; from stagecoach to automobiles; from buses to trains; from turbo props to jets.

None of these transformations changed the structure of the family unit. One could argue that they changed roles within the family unit, but not the fabric of the family unit.

There was a time when the family had one radio or TV for the whole family; and the father would decide what would be listened to or watched, thus it became an opportunity for the family to spend intimate time together.

There was a time that a family had one car for the whole family. During the week, typically the father used the car to go back and forth to work. On the weekends there would be family outings and of course, church on Sunday. Again, since there was only one car, this was another opportunity for family time.

In these instances, modernity changed the type and quality of time spent with the family, but not the composition of the family.

That all began to change with the rise of liberalism of the 1960s. President Johnson and the Democratic Congress began passing laws that would soon devastate the Black family and ultimately families in general.

Liberals in the 60s established what we now call welfare for girls who got pregnant without the benefit of being married. The only stipulations for receiving these government benefits was that you could not be married or have a male living in the same home. The government literally had social workers randomly showing up at your house to see if a male was present in the house. If they found a male living there or even male clothing in the closet, you would be immediately cut off from the programs. But, as long as you remained single you could stay on the programs for life. You would be given a free apartment, healthcare, and babysitting services—all for free, as long as you remained single, unemployed, and kept having babies.

The rise of the welfare state coincided with the rise of feminism, which basically said that a woman didn't need a man—once they got a man's sperm, he was totally irrelevant.

The convergence of the welfare state and feminism, has led to a prolonged assault on men and the traditional family unit.

Tyler Perry has made hundreds of millions of dollars from dressing like a woman in his movies; so has Martin Lawrence, Jaime Foxx, etc. My critics will say that this is just "acting." Oh really? Allow me to shed more light on the subject.

Two years ago, Morehouse College, one of the most esteemed Historically Black Colleges in the U.S (Martin Luther King attended), the president of the school had to send out a notice to the student body that the students were not allowed to were dresses or carry purses to class. You might be wondering what is so unusual about this. Well, Morehouse College is an all-male institution.

Now you have primary aged students being told that they have two mommies or two daddies; that is biologically impossible. You can only have one mother and one father.

This whole radical move to redefine the family will have disastrous results for the U.S. Name me one civilization or society that has thrived and prospered without an intact family structure. There are none.

The family unit is the DNA of a society. When you play around with a person's DNA, it leads to deformed children and in most cases; it is very expensive to medically treat people with genetic deformities.

It is not a coincidence that since the early 60s, the out of wedlock birthrate for Blacks is currently around 74%, Hispanics around 60%, and whites over 50%. There is direct causation between welfare, feminism and the destruction of or the marginalization of men and the family unit.

Men are the stabilizing influence in a boy's life and without that influence (that a woman cannot provide), you will see teenage pregnancy, crime, drug abuse, and every other negative pathology increase to epidemic proportions. When you have a man teaching a young boy how to be responsible and provide for his family; and the women teaching a young boy how to be nurturing; then and only then can you have a complete man.

But, this foolish notion that Tommy can have two dads or Susie can have two moms is akin to altering one's DNA; and all these societal problems we see are a direct result of this social engineering and attempted redefining of the family unit.

America had better put the brakes on this insidious experiment that is altering the DNA of America and the family.

CHAPTER 3

❧ SPORTS ❧

INTRODUCTION BY:

Michael "Scooter" McGruder, former N.F.L. cornerback and Chairman of Platinum Charities.

As a 12 year professional athlete in American football, I am thrilled that Raynard has chosen to utilize his weekly column to accentuate the positive in life, especially relative to professional athletes.

During our nearly 10 years of friendship, we have had many conversations about how professional athletes are portrayed in society and what their obligation to society should be. His piece on Tony McGee was very inspirational. In some ways, McGee was like the Rosa Parks of college football.

During my career, I have been fortunate enough to be recognized by my fellow players, as well as the community at large for trying to be the best person I could be, both on the field and off. I was recognized by the United Way with the Generation Excellence Award (for making an effort to improve the lives of others) and recognized as a finalist for the N.F.L.'s Bart Starr Award (given annually to an N.F.L. player who best exemplifies outstanding character and leadership in the home, on the field and in the community. This award was voted on by players throughout the league). These awards are just as meaningful to me as playing in Super Bowl XXXI with the New England Patriots.

In my view, professional athletes have an obligation to conduct themselves in a manner that will bring honor, not only to their sport, but also to their families.

Raynard's columns on Michael Vick were exceptional. He dealt with Vick's downfall and his ultimate redemption. Despite being celebrities, we athletes are still human; and Raynard's thoughtful way of writing about Vick as a human was remarkable.

Anyone who follows Raynard's writings knows he can also be very tough, as shown in his piece on golfer, Zakiya Randall. It is a very hard hitting piece, but I can't find any area where I disagree with him.

That is the beauty of Raynard's writing; it is hard-hitting, very insightful, and always thought provoking. I am so glad that he understands that most professional athletes are doing things the right way. I wish more of the public appreciated this fact.

America Has Gone To The Dogs

Published: June 18, 2009

What is this world coming to when a man that killed someone gets 30 days in jail, but a man that tortures a few dogs gets nearly two years in prison? American's have lost their minds!

Let me explain. On March 14, 2009, Donte Stallworth, a wide receiver for the Cleveland Browns of the National Football League (N.F.L.), struck and killed a pedestrian attempting to cross the street. It was determined that he was driving under the influence of alcohol (he had a blood alcohol of 0.12, Florida's legal limit is 0.08). So, he was legally drunk. He was charged with DUI and second degree manslaughter on April 1, 2009. On April 2, he turned himself in to the police and was released on $ 200,000 bail. Yesterday he pleaded guilty to all charges and received a sentence of 30 days in jail, 2 years of house arrest, 10 years of probation, permanent loss of his driver's license, and 1,000 hours of community service. Stallworth is reported to have also reached a financial agreement with the decedent's family (thereby avoiding a civil lawsuit). The terms of the settlement was not made public.

Now, flashback two years to Michael Vick. Vick was quarterback for the Atlanta Falcons of the N.F.L. In July 2007, Vick and three others were indicted on both federal and Virginia felony charges related to dog fighting. Vick was accused of financing the operation, directly participating in dog fights and executions, and personally handling thousands of dollars in gambling activities.

In early August, all of the defendants had agreed to individual plea deals with prosecutors. By August 24, according to media reports, Vick pled guilty to "Conspiracy to Travel in Interstate Commerce in Aid of Unlawful Activities and to Sponsor a Dog in an Animal Fighting Venture". In addition, he admitted to providing most of the financing for the operation itself, as well as participating directly in several dog fights in Virginia, Maryland, North Carolina and South Carolina. He also admitted to sharing in the proceeds from these dog fights.

He further admitted that he knew his colleagues killed several dogs that didn't perform well enough. However, while he admitted to providing most of the money for gambling on the fights, he denied placing any side bets on the dogfights. He also denied actually killing any dogs himself.

U.S. District Judge Henry E. Hudson accepted Vick's guilty plea the same day it was proffered. Hudson sentenced Vick to 23 months in federal prison. Vick was also required to deposit $1 million dollars into an escrow account to defray the costs associated with the caring and rehabilitation of the dogs used in his fighting operation.

Legally, I understand why and how these two cases were settled as they were. But, it just doesn't seem right that you can kill a person while drunk and get 30 days in jail. Someone else is involved in dog fighting and gets 23 months in jail.

Legality aside, what does this say about our country when a person is killed and no public outrage (not even from the victim's family). Kill and abuse a few dogs and it's a media circus! People were talking about dogs as though they were humans. But, these same people won't raise their voice at the death of a human.

Now, all the talk is whether N.F.L. Commissioner Roger Goodell will reinstate Vick to play football again. According to USA Today, Goodell stated that Vick must show "genuine remorse" before he will be allowed to play in the N.F.L. again. Goodell continued, "he's going to have to demonstrate to the larger community—not just to the N.F.L. community and to me—that he has remorse for what he did and that he recognizes mistakes that he made."

How do you prove remorse? Isn't that kind of like "knowing pornography" when you see it? Vick has paid his debt to society and is entitled to move on and continue with his football career (if a team wants him).

But, there are other clouds on the horizon for Vick. Earlier this year in a local Virginia newspaper, People for the Ethical Treatment of Animals (PETA) President, Ingrid Newkirk stated, "Saying sorry and getting his ball back after being caught enjoying killing dogs in hideously cruel ways for many years doesn't cut it. Commissioner Goodell knows that he has an obligation to the league and to millions of fans, including children who look up to ballplayers as idols."

There is absolutely no evidence that Vick "killed or enjoyed" being cruel to dogs. Vick simply made poor choices. Again, he as paid his dues to society and PETA needs to back off and show the same type of concern for humans who are mistreated, tortured, or killed.

Michael Is A "Vick-tim"

Published: July 29, 2009

Michael Vick has become the "Vick-tim" of his own choices and at the same time a victim of America's hypocrisy.

Vick (the Vick-tim) put himself in the position where he had to do time in prison. He was always made to feel above the law from his days at Virginia Tech. This led to his arrogance to the point where he felt he did not have to listen to anyone.

But at the same time, Vick has become the victim of our hypocrisy. Putting aside all legal considerations, I am appalled at how people are outraged that he killed a few dogs. But these same people don't lift a voice at all the teenagers who have been killed in Chicago this year alone! Even those who feel Vick has served his time feel compelled to preface their statements with, "I love dogs or what Vick did was wrong." I am tired of everyone trying to be politically correct (PC).

Let me make my point CLEAR, I don't give a damn about these dogs! What does this say about our country that we get more upset over dogs than we do over human life?

Roger Goodell has conditionally reinstated Vick to the N.F.L. (with all kinds of stipulations), but it seems like everyone is piling on. Vick served nearly two years in jail, lost multiple millions of dollars in endorsement deals, and filed for bankruptcy. How much more should one person have to pay back to society?

Now, juxtapose that with Dante Stallworth, a receiver with the Cleveland Browns. Earlier this year he pleaded guilty to DUI and second degree manslaughter. He was sentenced to 30 days in jail (only served 24 because of good behavior), 1,000 hours of community service, 8 years of probation, 2 years of house arrest, and life-time suspension of his driver's license. And he killed a human!

There were no protests in the street, no picketing of N.F.L. headquarters, or no boycotting of advertisers. So, do you honestly think a damn dog is more valuable than a human life?

Stallworth has been indefinitely suspended from football, but probably will be allowed to play after one year if he stays clear of further legal issues.

Again, Vick put himself in the position he is in and has no one to blame but himself. But, he has become the poster child and a convenient target for America's hypocrisy. Even the murder of the couple in Florida who adopted all the handicapped kids, didn't cause the level of outrage as Vick killing a few dogs.

Vick has suffered enough and deserves a second chance. Whether you agree with his actions are not, he has paid his debt to society and should not be required to work with the Humane Society or any other group unless he chooses to. He is doing all these things strictly to get back into football.

Martha Stewart is back on TV (insider trading), Oliver North (lying to Congress about Iran Contra) is back on the radio, and Marv Albert (rape) is back in broadcasting. You never hear any mention of their crimes anymore. They have been allowed to get back into their professional fields and make lots of money without the public being constantly reminded of their past transgressions. I think Vick deserves the same treatment.

My whole point is proportionality and fairness. Again, legal considerations aside, how do you justify putting Vick through all the BS he is going through over a few dogs? The justice view is that Vick put himself in this situation;

the fairness view is that he is a victim of America's hypocrisy!

A Rolle Model

Published: May 6, 2010

E ven non-sports fans have heard of athletes like Terrell Owens (T.O.), "Pacman" Jones, Mike Tyson, O. J. Simpson or Ben Roethlisberger—for all the wrong reasons. But, I guarantee that most people have never heard of Myron Rolle.

Who is Myron Rolle? He is a recent Rhodes Scholar who is finishing his graduate degree in medical anthropology. He graduated from Florida State University (FSU) in 2 ½ years with a pre-medical degree in exercise science (with a grade point average of 3.75).

So, why is this so newsworthy? Let me continue. He decided to forego his senior year of football eligibility to accept a Rhodes Scholarship and attend graduate school at Oxford University in England. There are only 32 Rhodes Scholarships awarded every year. He played football for three years at one of the best football schools in the country—FSU. He gave up his senior year to attend graduate school, thereby deferring by one year his dream of playing professional football (had he entered the draft instead of going to Oxford, he was projected to go in either the 1st or 2nd round).

Rolle has already stated that after his career in professional football, he plans to attend medical school to become a neurosurgeon. To that end, he has already established his own foundation—the Myron L. Rolle Medical Clinic and Sports Complex (www.myronrolle.com). The clinic will be built in Steventon, Exuma in the Bahamas (where Rolle's parents are from). Rolle grew up in Galloway, New Jersey.

Last month, Rolle was drafted in the 6th round by the Tennessee Titans as the 207th overall selection. There were a total of 7 rounds and 255 people drafted. What I find fascinating is why Rolle was drafted so low.

According to several media reports, during the N.F.L.'s annual spring combines (where all the top college prospects work out for team executives); the word was that Rolle was not committed to football. This was because he passed up his senior year to go to graduate school. So, let me get this right—because Rolle is smart and his life consists of more than just playing football, he somehow is not committed to being a good professional football player?

This type of thinking among N.F.L. executives led to one of the most offensive situations I have ever heard of in professional sports. At the Senior Bowl last January, Rolle had a pre-draft interview with the staff of the Tampa Bay Buccaneers, including the head coach (Raheem Morris, the youngest coach in the league—33-- and Black) and general manager Mark Dominik. During this meeting, a member of the coaching staff asked Rolle what it felt like to desert his team to attend graduate school? Rolle later told a reporter, "I hadn't heard that one before. My initial reaction was a bit of confusion. " So, he was chosen lower in the draft because he is a smart, well rounded person who is already planning for a future without football. What message is this sending to our youth? One N.F.L. executive is quoted as having said, "he's a better story than he is a player."

According to Rolle, "The impression I get from people around the NFL – not necessarily in it, but around it – is that the NFL wants players for whom football is their No. 1 priority, their No. 2 priority and their No. 3 priority...For me, I've never been someone with a singular talent. I have other abilities and interests and I think I would be doing a disservice to me, my team, my family, everyone who has invested stock in me if I was just so isolated in one thing. ... The thing I always try to present to people in the NFL as far as my commitment is that my academics and my concerns at Oxford or as an outside philanthropist can help my football abilities. It can help me be someone more disciplined on the field, help me be someone more balanced and knowledgeable. It can help the other guys if they want to get involved in the foundation or the community rather than going out and partying or getting in trouble somehow."

There was no public outcry when the story about Tampa Bay became public. But, let an athlete be suspended for a few games for getting into trouble with the law and people lose their minds.

Has our society really come to the point where being intelligent is now a liability and can actually cause you to be drafted in a later round because your commitment to the game is now in question?

Myron Rolle should be universally lauded and praised for showing us that you don't have to smart or an athlete; but you can be both. I find it ironic that at 6'2" and 215 lbs, Rolle plays the safety position. The safety is the last line of defense before the opponent scores a touchdown. He truly is the last line of defense against the caricature of the "dumb" athlete. Right before our eyes, Myron is playing the role of a lifetime, but it doesn't' seem like he has much of a supporting cast. But, if he continues down the path he is on, his choices will be vindicated and he will be viewed as the ultimate Rolle model.

Michael Vick—From Vick-tim to Vick-tory

Published:December 2, 2010

A m I the only one who is sick and tired of the media coverage of NFL quarterback Michael Vick—post incarceration? Last July I wrote a column titled, "Michael Is A Vick-tim." I discussed Vick's going to jail for nearly two years for killing a couple of dogs.

He has served his time and is now playing football again in the NFL. He has had a stellar season as the starting quarterback for the Philadelphia Eagles. Since leaving jail earlier this year, he has done all the right things and continues to speak out against animal cruelty on behalf of the Humane Society.

So, you ask, what am I angry about?

Why is it that every time Vick is interviewed on radio, TV, or newspaper, there has to be some mention of him serving jail time for killing dogs? ENOUGH! Vick has served his time and owes no one anything and he should be free to live his life beyond the shadow of his past.

As I reflected on Vick's situation, the first thought I had was that this was because Vick was Black. But, then I thought further and realized that it wasn't about race.

Ray Lewis, future Hall of Fame linebacker for the Baltimore Ravens, was jailed on murder charges in 2000, but was later acquitted. You rarely if ever hear this being mentioned when Lewis is interviewed. He is also Black.

You never hear the name Monica Lewinsky when Bill Clinton is interviewed (mind you that Bill Clinton was impeached as a result of the Lewinsky affair).

You never hear about Donald Trump's many bankruptcies when he is interviewed.

Allow me to continue.

Diana Taurasi, an all-star guard of the Phoenix Mercury of the WNBA, was convicted of DUI in the summer of 2009. I have never heard this mentioned during any of their games on TV.

Marv Albert, famed NBA TV announcer, pled guilty to misdemeanor assault and battery charges (the more serious charge of rape was dropped). He was fired from announcing the games on NBC. But, less than 2 years later, NBC rehired him and you have not heard one word about his conviction since.

Even Tiger Woods messy divorce is no longer discussed when talking about Woods and it's only been barely over a year since his private life exploded onto the national scene.

So, what can we conclude about all this?

Well, it seem to me that if you are a celebrity and you commit a crime or violent act against another person—no problem. If you cheat your bankers or file for bankruptcy, no problem. You still will be considered a financial guru by the Wall Street Journal (i.e. Donald Trump).

But, God forbid you kill or torture a few animals! You will never be forgiven, nor allowed to move beyond your past; even if your life shows a total change.

How can a sportscaster laud Michael Vick throwing an acrobatic touchdown pass, but yet somehow find a way to mention that Vick served time in jail?

How can Vick have arguably one of the best games in football history (3 weeks ago against the Washington Redskins) and the conversation turns to him abusing animals?

Vick has paid his dues to society and no longer owes anyone anything! His life has been the model of redemption. That should be the only relevance of Vick's past.

But, because Vick's crime centered around animals, it seems like people are less willing to forgive and let go. Ray Lewis was implicated in the murder of a human, but it seems like he had an easier time moving beyond his transgression than Vick is having.

Donte Stallworth (receiver for the Baltimore Ravens) was convicted of manslaughter. He killed a man while driving drunk. Yet, he is shown more forgiveness than Vick.

So, Michael, let me offer you my advice as one who works in public relations. First, Michael, stop apologizing. You no longer owe society anything. Second, tell the media you will no longer talk about your past. When you were a child, you spoke as a child, but now that you are a man, you have put those childish things behind you. Finally, Michael, when the media insists that you answer their questions about your past, simply say my life is the only voice that I am now speaking with.

I am very proud of Michael Vick and the distance he has traveled. I hope he will win a Super Bowl ring before his career is over. What an exclamation point that would add to his life. We all are one bad decision away from doing something stupid. If Vick continues to live his life the way he has since getting out of prison, he will have transformed his life from one of being a "Vick-tim to one of "Vick-tory."

McGee and the Wyoming 14

Published: February 3, 2011

With the beginning of Black History Month two days ago and the upcoming Super Bowl on Sunday, I thought I would bring you a story that has gotten very little attention, especially in the Washington, DC area.

How many of you are familiar with former professional football player Tony McGee (Washington Redskins) and the Wyoming 14? It's very unfortunate that most of you have never heard of either. They represent everything good about a previous generation that made significant contributions to the freedom and luxuries that we enjoy today.

In many ways, they were the "Rosa Parks" of the Pacific Northwest in the U.S.

College and professional athletes often get a bad rap for the way they behave, both on and off the field. A lot of the criticism is justified, but most athletes are model citizens and never get in any trouble. They go through life just like the rest of us.

Former British Prime Minister, Winston Churchill once stated, "To every man, there comes a time when he is figuratively tapped on the shoulder and offered the chance to do a great and mighty work; unique to him and fitted to his talents; what a tragedy if that moment finds him unprepared or unqualified for the moment that could be his finest hour."

On Oct. 17, 1969, Tony McGee and the Wyoming 14 received their tap on the shoulder.

That was the day all 14 Black players were kicked off the University of Wyoming's football team by their coach-- Lloyd Eaton.

This was all precipitated by Willie Black, head of the Black Student Alliance (BSA). Earlier in the week he had sent a letter to the school asking the university and other Western Athletic Conference (WAC) members not to schedule games with Brigham Young University (BYU) until the Mormon Church rescinded its racist policies towards Blacks (they were not allowed to become priests, strictly based on their race).

After the BSA meeting, Joe Williams (running back) had asked the coach if it would be OK for him and the other 13 Black players to wear a black armband during the upcoming Saturday game against BYU. The players also wanted to protest the usage of racial epithets by BYU during last year's game. Williams was a tri-captain on the team. Eaton gave Williams an emphatic "NO," claiming the action would violate a team rule prohibiting any type of demonstration. So, the players attempted to change the coach's mind by going to meet with him in his office wearing their armbands. Eaton led them to the bleachers in the old field house, where he immediately dismissed them from the team.

According to McGee (defensive end), "He said we could go to Grambling State or Morgan State... We could go back to colored relief (welfare). If anyone said anything, he told us to shut up. We were really protesting policies we thought were racist. Maybe we should've been protesting there."

The next day, October 18, 1969, the university president, board of trustees and governor upheld the coach's decision. A civil case seeking restitution for the players was in court for three years before being denied.

Wyoming never recovered from the loss of the 14 athletes. Before they were kicked off the team, Wyoming was off to a 4-0 start and was ranked # 10 in the country. They ended the season with a 6-4 record and didn't have another winning season until 1976 and didn't play in another bowl game until 1987.

Coach Eaton resigned at the end of the following season— with a 1-9 record. According to media accounts, Eaton never discussed the incident again, except with his wife, Dolly. According to her, "He was not bitter... He had a good conscience about it... "All the people thought like he did. You should not make fun or criticize another religion." Eaton died in 2007 at the age of 88.

Because of the actions of these 14 Black players, BYU signed their first Black player in 1970 (Bennie Smith) and in 1978 the Mormon Church reversed its policy on Blacks in the priesthood.

McGee went on to finish his college career and received his degree from Bishop College (a Black college in Dallas). According to McGee, he was scheduled to be a first round draft pick, but he ended up going in the third round (64th pick) to the Chicago Bears in the 1971 NFL draft. Word was sent out throughout the NFL, that McGee was part of the Wyoming 14 and was a trouble maker.

He played 14 seasons in the NFL and played in back to back Super Bowls with the Washington Redskins, winning one and losing one.

In 1985, McGee's created his own TV show called, "Pro Football Plus," a weekly sports show that he hosts.

Unfortunately, when coach Lloyd Eaton was tapped on the shoulder; he was found unprepared for the moment that could have been his finest hour.

Fortunately, McGee and his 13 teammates were well prepared for a time that proved to be their finest hour.

So, as we prepare to watch the upcoming Super Bowl, please take a few moments to reflect upon the sacrifice McGee and his teammates made. I have included a couple of links below for those who want to find out more about this moment in history.

http://www.youtube.com/watch?v=bljO4ovARZQ   (made by a 13 year old)

http://uwacadweb.uwyo.edu/robertshistory/fired_by_conscience.htm

Shaquille O'Neal, the Center of Attention

Published: June 9, 2011

L ast week, N.B.A. great Shaquille O'Neal announced his retirement after 19 years of playing professional basketball. He stood 7'1" and weighed over 325 pounds (depending on the day of the week). He was one of the biggest people to ever play the game.

He left Louisiana State University (LSU) after 3 years to join the N.B.A. He was picked as the number 1 player in 1992 draft by the Orlando Magic. He was chosen as the rookie of the year and went on to become one of the most dominant centers in the history of the game.

Shaq won 4 championships, 3 with the Los Angeles Lakers and 1 with the Miami Heat. If you want to read more about his basketball accomplishments, just Google him.

All of sports has been buzzing about his retirement and paying homage to him and his career. But, my faithful readers know that I am constantly looking for a different angle when writing about an issue. Shaq's retirement is no different.

Shaq had one of the most endearing personalities you will ever encounter. Beneath all the humor was a man of great seriousness. The times we were together, we had very engaging conversations, mixed with a lot of wild humor.

He used his sense of humor to make people comfortable with him because, at his height and weight, he was a very imposing figure. Because of this affability, he has one of the most extensive rolodexes of any athlete anywhere. Even in retirement, he can pick up the phone and call some of the most influential people from the worlds of business, politics, sports and entertainment.

He planned for his retirement with his personality. He has made over $ 300 million in his career (this does not include well over $ 100 million in various endorsement deals), so money should not be an issue with him. But, because he used his personality to build relationships, he has the whole world at his fingertips.

With his many championships, with his larger than life personality, and with all the people he knows; there is one thing about him that stands out with me more than anything else. It's the one thing you rarely, if ever, hear mentioned when talking about Shaq.

After leaving LSU in 1992, Shaq eventually earned his college degree in 2000, receiving a BA in General Studies. But, he didn't stop there. He went on to earn his M.B.A. in

2005 from the University of Phoenix. But, he didn't stop there. He is currently pursuing his Ph.D in Leadership and Education with a specialization in Human Resource Development from Barry University in Florida.

So, don't be fooled by Shaq's crazy sense of humor. Behind the humor is a highly motivated person who is striving to make himself a better person away from the game of basketball.

With all the money he has, he didn't need to finish his degree from LSU and surely didn't need the advanced degrees. But, his educational pursuits are about self-actualization—being the best he can be for self-empowerment.

I found an interesting, but sad anecdote about Shaq. When I Googled "Shaquille O'Neal," I got 9.2 million hits. But, when I Googled "Shaquille O'Neal and education," I got 2.69 million hits. So, there are almost 4 times as many references to Shaq's basketball career than there is to his educational accomplishments. What a shame!

If Shaq were pulled over by the police for driving while intoxicated, it would be all over the news. So, if Shaq had run afoul of the law, the media would be giving him the 3rd degree; but there is hardly a mention of him pursuing his 3rd degree!

For this accomplishment, Shaq deserves to be the center of attention.

From Vick-tim to Victory Part II

Published: September 15, 2011

L ast December, I wrote a column titled, "Michael Vick--From Vick-tim to Vick-tory." The premise of that piece was that Vick made poor decisions which ultimately caused him to serve time in a federal prison. After leaving prison, his lifestyle suggested that he had truly turned his life around. This again involved Vick making decisions that impacted his life. So, almost a year later, I wanted to write a piece to update my readers on this wonderful story.

Last year's piece focused on what Vick did to cause his troubles and how his decisions (post prison) could lead to him moving beyond his troubles.

Vick had a phenomenal season for the Philadelphia Eagles last year. In fact, he was named to the Pro Bowl (and picked as the starting quarterback for the NFC), named by Associated Press & Sporting News as the comeback player of the year, and was runner up for the Most Valuable Player (MVP) of the league.

Yet, there are still those who want to continue to deny Vick his right to make a living and move on with his life. If you have that much of a problem with Vick, then just don't watch him play football; but please let those of us who believe in redemption continue to enjoy and be a witness to this inspiring story taking place right before our very eyes.

Vick has continued to work with the Humane Society to educate people about animal cruelty. He has continued to speak to students about making good life choices. He seems to have truly turned his life around and is a testament to those who have made mistakes.

We all make mistakes, but through our actions, we can show that lessons have been learned through those mistakes. That's what maturity and wisdom are all about.

I do hope someone will do a movie about Vick's journey. His journey can be an inspiration to us all, no matter how big or small the mistake. Just like one makes a decision to do something bad; that same process can make one reform one's life to gain the victory over one's circumstances.

Vick's victory has been so complete that in July of this year Nike signed him to another endorsement deal. This is unprecedented! This is the first time a major sponsor has ever resigned an athlete they had previously dropped.

Just last month, Vick signed a 6-year, $100 million contract with the Eagles, with $ 40 million guaranteed.

Vick's turnaround is nothing short of miraculous. Though he is in bankruptcy financially, this new contract, along with the steady stream of endorsements, should allow Vick to regain his financial footing.

But, more important than the money, Vick has developed into a "MAN." His conversation is different, his game is different, and his life is different. He is now the unquestioned leader of his team, his family, and his life.

He is almost like a person who has cheated death. People like this tend to have a new take on life and those things that are most important.

Football has helped him make a living, but his past has helped him make a life. These are truly the things that turn boys to men.

So, Mike, you are no longer a "Vick-tim," you are a "Vick-tor." Because you have learned from your past, defeat has been swallowed up in VICTORY!

Jimmy Graham--A True Baller

Published: October 27, 2011

That's right, Jimmy Graham! Most of the public is only recently becoming aware of the story of Jimmy Graham. I find this very unfortunate, but true.

Jimmy Graham is a tight end for the New Orleans Saints football team. As of this writing, he is the leading tight end in the N.F.L. in terms of receptions and touchdowns. But most importantly, he is proving to be a true "baller" in the game of life!

He was born and raised in Greensboro, North Carolina. This 24 year old has scored big both on and off the field. Just imagine, at the age of 11, being put in a parent's car and then being dropped off at an orphanage.

Well, unfortunately for Graham, he doesn't have to imagine this—this was his life. Graham recounts the story of him being in the back seat of a van with his housemates from the orphanage and being beaten until his eyes were swollen shut. He called his mother and asked her to pick him up and she simply hung up the phone. Ouch!

After bouncing around from house to house, he was eventually taken into the home of his future adoptive mother, Becky Vinson during his high school years.

According to Graham, he and his biological mother are "slowly rebuilding a relationship, but it's moving very slowly…I told her that I forgive her, but I won't forget."

Graham is a better man than I am. I am very impressed with the way he presents himself on TV. But, his attitude towards his mother goes to the type of character he has. Isn't it a shame that more people are aware of Beyonce's pregnancy than Graham's story?

Graham, who now stands 6'6" and 260 pounds, earned a basketball scholarship to attend the University of Miami (commonly referred to as "The U"). He played football in his last year of school (along with four years of basketball).

He graduated in 2009 with a double major in marketing and management. He then enrolled in graduate school so he could play one year of football. During the 2010 NFL Draft, Graham was picked by the New Orleans Saints in the third round (95th overall pick). He was signed to a four year, $ 2.5 million contract.

There is a lot more to this story, but because of space constraints, there is not enough room to write about everything; but just Google his name and you can read all the details of this fascinating person.

So, the next time you hear or read a negative story about a professional athlete, just think about Michael Vick or Jimmy Graham.

Most professional athletes are good, upstanding citizens. Don't allow the media to cloud your views because of a few bad apples.

Jimmy Graham's story makes you cry, makes you angry, and makes you joyful.

You can't help but cry when you think of the traumatic experience he suffered at the age of 11. You can't help but be angry at how an adult and a mother could subject her own child to such a life altering situation. But, you can't help but be joyful about how an 11 year old, traumatized kid could develop into such a wonderful, marvelous person!

This story is not about sports, it's about life. We all have faced or will face our own traumatic situation(s) in our life. How we respond will determine the quality of our life.

There are not many people who I really want to meet in life, but Jimmy Graham is definitely one. I want to know how he went from failing grades, to a basketball scholarship to a very prominent university (with a double major in marketing and management), finished in four years, then enrolled in graduate school so he could play one year of football, and then to excel on the professional level in football. All this while overcoming the trauma of his youth.

Jimmy Graham, your life is truly a touchdown. Whether you know it or not, you have already won the Super Bowl of life!

Zakiya Randall Is Not Up To Par

Published: May 18, 2012

Former British Prime Minister, Winston Churchill, once said, "To every man there comes a time when he is figuratively tapped on the shoulder and offered the chance to do a great and mighty work; unique to him and fitted to his talents; what a tragedy if that moment finds him unprepared or unqualified for the moment that could be his finest hour."

Zakiya Randall has been tapped on the shoulder and has proven that she is woefully unprepared and unqualified for the moment that could be her finest hour!

Randall is a 20 year old, Arlington, VA native, now residing in Atlanta. She is supposed to be an up and coming golf prodigy. But, this column is less about her golf and more about her person.

Randall is a very attractive girl, who definitely has great potential; but, unfortunately, I would be very surprised if this potential was ever realized because she seems to want to be a sex object more than a golfer.

Her arrogance is astonishing and very repulsive! She is young and brash, with none of the hardware (winning titles) to back up her bravado. In some ways, she reminds me of Michelle Wie (the former teenage golfer who was pushed too hard and too fast by parents who wanted to live vicariously through her). But, at least Wie's parents refused to let their daughter be used as a sex object.

Wie has a very well done website and it is filled with Fortune 500 companies as sponsors. (http://www.michellewie.com) Her photo pages are filled with very tasteful, beautiful pictures of her, both on the golf course and away from the golf course. Wie went from a highly exposed teenager with lots of money and fame, to a seemingly classy adult who will receive her degree from Stanford University this month (with a degree in communications). Wie has accomplished all this without being sexually objectified.

You may now be asking, what I am talking about? Please view this video and you will understand my rant very clearly (http://www.golfchannel.com/media/big-break-atlantis-zakiya-bio-041012/).

When I saw this video, I was totally disgusted at Randall, and even more so with her parents. Why would a parent allow their daughter to be so sexually objectified? But, more importantly, what was it about Randall and her parents that made the Golf Channel comfortable shooting a video showing various close-up shots, in slow motion, of Randall's private parts?

None of the other girls in this video were shot in this manner. Randall is the only Black girl in this video and on this particular Golf Channel TV show. Why are Black women content to allow themselves to constantly be debased in the most public of manner? Why am I seemingly more upset at this constant sexual objectification of Black women than Black women?

Randall is managed by her mother, so ultimately they both agreed to let this be done. Randall thinks she can make money by being sexually exploited. Correction, sexually used. Exploitation indicates coercion. Well, obviously, it's not working. When you go to her website, it is clumsily put together and cluttered with the most egotistical verbiage I have ever seen. There are no major corporate sponsors. I wonder why?

Randall is just another in a recent string of Black women who bring shame on themselves and women in general. Last year, I wrote a piece titled "Black Women No Longer Have Their Essence." This piece was about the "Basketball Wives" craze and the "Housewives of Atlanta" craze. As if the shows weren't bad enough, Essence Magazine honored some of the women involved in both shows.

Please, I don't want to hear anything about Randall being young (20). Wie was young also, but no network ever showed close-ups of her private parts! The only difference being that of parenting.

Wei's parents emigrated from South Korea to Hawaii (where Wei was born). Asians typically raise their children in a very conservative manner, with a clear delineation of authority within the home. They are taught that education is the key to their future. Thus, Wei will be receiving her college degree from Stanford University this month and Randall is not even in school.

Randall and her parents need help. Beautiful, she is. Talented, she is. Smart, she is not. She is old enough to know better, but if she was raised in an environment to believe that being sexually objectified is ok; then, I blame her parents.

Randall either has no professional PR people around her or she simply is not listening to their advice. In either case, she is embarrassing herself and Black women. She needs to be reined in. If she wants to be famous, try winning! I know, what a novel concept.

If Randall doesn't tone down her cockiness and stop allowing herself to be sexually objectified, she will become the most recent child prodigy that is enshrined in the hall of anonymity. She truly has been tapped on the shoulder, but what a tragedy that she has been found unqualified and unprepared for the moment that could have been her finest hour.

Junior Bridgeman: From The NBA Hardwood To The Boardroom

Published: September 5, 2012

So often in today's media, professional athletes are caricatured as dumb, narcissistic, spoiled brats who know the cost of everything and the value of nothing. In today's world of sports, if you are not chest-bumping or causing some other attention to be drawn to yourself, you are considered boring.

In today's celebrity obsessed society, people know who is pregnant, the baby's name, who is sleeping with whom, etc. Strangely enough, today, you can be famous for being famous—with no accomplishments to speak of.

But, yet, "old-school" success has never gone out of vogue, it's just been ignored. Everyone knows Michael Jordan and

Earvin "Magic" Johnson, but who knows Ulysses Lee "Junior" Bridgeman?

Typical measures of success are how much money you make, how many gold records you have, or how many championships you have won. But, my measure of success is the distance travelled from where you began.

Bridgeman played 12 years in the National Basketball Association (NBA)—10 years for the Milwaukee Bucks and 2 years for the Los Angeles Clippers. He was born in East Chicago, Indiana and played college ball (and graduated) at the University of Louisville. His father was a blue collar steel mill worker, as was very common in that part of the country during the 60s.

Bridgeman was considered a very good, steady player and was able to make a good living playing basketball. Mind you, Bridgeman's professional basketball career spanned from 1975 to 1987, well before players were paid the exorbitant money they are now paid. He retired right before players started to make the big money.

Though Michael Jordan made the bulk of his money from endorsement deals, he still made close to $ 100 million in salary from the NBA alone. Bridgeman never made anywhere close to that type of money. Magic Johnson probably made even more money than Jordan from salary alone, being in LA.

With that as my premise, I would argue that Bridgeman is more successful than either Jordan or Johnson. Not so much in terms of money (though he is estimated to be worth well over $ 200 million), but in terms of where he started. The NBA helped him make a living, but his morals and values helped him make a life.

His company, Bridgeman Foods LLC, operates over 160 Wendy's hamburger restaurants (he is the second largest Wendy's franchisee in the world). He also owns over 118 Chili's restaurants. He has over 11,000 employees and revenues in excess of $ 500 million. He is listed as one of the top 20 "Richest Black Americans," according to Forbes Magazine and is ranked # 3 on the Restaurant Finance Monitor's Top 200 franchisee-owned companies. An avid golfer, he also sits on the board of directors of the Professionals Golfers Association (PGA).

While his fellow athletes were hanging out during the off season, Bridgeman was working in local Wendy's restaurants, learning the business from top to bottom. Again, basketball helped him make a living.

But, his wife of 34 years, Doris has helped him make a life. They have three adult children (Justin, Ryan, and

Eden) and all are working in the family business. Both Justin and Ryan have MBAs and Eden is in preparation for hers.

Last month, I profiled another successful businessman, David Steward of World Wide Technology (http://www.blackenterprise.com/news-politics/moral-success/). He and Bridgeman are identical twins, as far as their approach to business is concerned. They both have been married to their respective wives for over 30 years and both believe you can be a successful businessman and a Christian at the same time. They are not mutually exclusive. Why has TV One or BET never profiled Blacks who made their money in industries other than sports and entertainment?

Bridgeman is a very private person, but I would hope that he will allow more people the privilege of meeting someone of this stature and to share the beauty of how you can raise a beautiful family, earn an honest living and have a good life.

CHAPTER 4
❧ POLITICS ❧

INTRODUCTION BY:

Trent Lott, Principal, The Breaux Lott Leadership Group and former Majority Leader of the United States Senate.

I have known Raynard for almost two decades and am flattered that he asked me to write the introduction to the Politics section of his book.

As Senate Majority Leader, I often sought him out for his advice and guidance on various pieces of legislation, as well as on political issues. Other times he sought me out and gave me his thoughts whether I asked or not!

His insightful political acumen is borne out in his columns. As Majority Leader, you are inundated with information, so brevity is always an asset when communicating with someone in my position.

I find Raynard's columns to be very concise and straight to the point. I look forward to reading his columns because they give me a very unique perspective into current affairs. My wish is that the Republican Party better utilizes him and his unique perspective to help the party get better traction within the Black community.

During my last election in Mississippi, I received 38% of the Black vote because I took the time to build relations with the Black community throughout my state.

I think Raynard has rightly criticized our party for not doing more to communicate our message to the Black community. His analysis is right on target and many of his recommendations should be implemented.

One of my favorite columns by Raynard is, "What it Means to be an American." As is always the case, this column is well written, but just as important is Raynard succinctly captured the essence of what it means to be an American.

In America, you can take someone born in the heartland of America (St. Louis, MO) and someone born in the Deep South (Grenada, MS) and they both become friends by trying to make America a better place by promoting good conservative values.

In today's world of politics, you don't have many true friends; but Raynard has proven to be a dear friend to Tricia and me.

Rosa Parks—Standing Tall by Sitting Down

Published: October 27, 2005

Though Rosa Parks died Monday night, her life and legacy will continue to live on for years to come. She deserves all the accolades she is receiving, but most don't realize that she was not the first to refuse to give up her seat.

Several months before Parks, 15-year-old Claudette Colvin did the same thing in the same city. One day in 1955, Colvin and three other black women sitting in the middle of a bus were asked to give up their seats to white passengers. Two did, but Colvin and an elderly woman refused. When the bus driver called the police, the elderly woman fled. Colvin refused to run. She bravely waited for the police to arrest her.

After police took Colvin away in handcuffs, some activists considered using this case as their catalyst to attack segregated seating on busses. They learned Ms. Colvin was pregnant and unmarried, and they feared that putting her in the spotlight would give blacks a bad image. They also feared the larger community would not support a pregnant teenager and therefore would not support her cause to end segregation.

Later that same year, Rosa Parks followed Colvin's example of brave defiance, refused to yield her seat to a white passenger, and got arrested just as Colvin did. This time, civil rights activists such as E.D. Nixon and Martin Luther King rallied behind Parks and finally launched the boycott they had considered launching over the Colvin arrest.

Now, the NAACP had their model plaintiff and King was the movement's perfect leader who would lead the bus boycott. The boycott lasted for 381 days.

King later wrote that Parks had become "a victim of both the forces of history and the forces of destiny." The boycott's led to the 1964 Civil Rights Act, which banned racial discrimination in public accommodations.

So, we all stand on the shoulders of Claudette Colvin **and** Rosa Parks. But what I find sad and embarrassing is how we in the Black community allow our icons to suffer in their later years.

Ms. Parks had a series of high profile legal and financial problems in her later years. Her foundation's van was repossessed, the IRS placed liens her foundation's property for failure to pay taxes, she was threatened with eviction several times from her home, etc.

I separate her business affairs from her personal affairs. Where was Jesse, Al, etc. when she was threatened with eviction? She should have never been in such a tenable situation to begin with. Where were all the athletes and entertainers who constantly invoked her name at awards ceremonies? Why didn't she have a modest house bought and paid for years ago? She should have had a trust fund set up specifically to take care of her living expenses for life.

Why is it that we allow our icons to suffer embarrassments in their later years? Joe Lewis (ended up being a doorman at a Las Vegas Casino), Redd Foxx (IRS put a lien on and repossessed all his belongings), Ron Isley (lost his music catalogue that was auctioned off to Michael Bolton because of back taxes), Sammie Davis, Jr. (and his wife Altovise) died in financial ruin, (it was Frank Sinatra who gave her $ 1 million in cash after the funeral), etc. Yeah, some of their embarrassments were self-inflicted, but at a minimum, the beneficiaries of their work should have stood up to make sure at least they had a roof over their heads and food on the table.

Can you think of any other race of people who allows their elders to suffer such embarrassments? African culture dictates that you take care of them. Name the last trailblazer of Jewish decent to end their years in such a manner.

By allowing her to go through her last years in such a manner and not standing up for her, Jesse, Al, Louie, please sit down!

Obama Drama

Published: March 26, 2009

L ast year, President Barack Obama ran the closest thing to a perfect campaign ever seen in this country. There was no senior level turnover during the campaign. There was no public feuding from various factions within his campaign (unlike Hillary Clinton's). Even the transition was extraordinarily smooth.

So, I am dumbfounded by all the drama surrounding the early days of his presidency. Seems like Obama went from a serious drama to a sitcom in short order. When he made his announcement in Springfield, IL in 2007, it was **All in the Family**, with his wife and children. The media portrayed him as the ultimate **Family Guy**. He campaigned **One Day at a Time** with his cast of **Friends**.

He campaigned with a discipline unseen in presidential politics. With his upset victory in the Iowa caucuses, his supporters were feeling **Good Times**. But with the unexpected loss in New Hampshire, they felt **Bewitched and Lost**. But, he proved to be a **Survivor** heading into Super Tuesday.

He refused to take his campaign into the **Weeds**, even when Hillary's campaign went very negative on him. For that, he received **Big Love** from the voters. The Obama campaign got hit with **The Facts of Life** of politics as the Clinton's showed their true **Colors** in South Carolina. Bill Clinton basically said welcome to **The Real World**. Obama tried to knock Hillary out in Texas, but they went down to the **Wire**. But, he did ultimately destroy the Clinton's **Dynasty**. They never thought he could win **The Office**. Their explanation was definitely from **Spin City**.

The Democratic convention was one of the best run conventions ever. The huge crowds gave him loud **Cheers,** thereby making him an **American Idol**. During the general election, Obama ran an **Amazing Race**, with John McCain being the **Biggest Loser**. His campaign made McCain's team look like a bunch of **Scrubs** and subsequently, they all disappeared **Without a Trace**.

Now that Obama made his **Bones**, it was time to move to the **West Wing**. He found that it was a **Different World** than he thought. He inherited an economy that was in the **General Hospital**, but is now in the **ER**.

There is no doubt that Obama has one of **America's Toughest Jobs**. But, with **20/20** hindsight, it's quite obvious that his budget will turn our country into a **Supernanny** state. As the **World Turns** and Obama searches for his **Guiding Light**, our country seems to see nothing but **Dark Shadows**.

Seems the **Commander in Chief** wants us to live on **Fantasy Island**—a place where the government is the answer to all that ails us.

But **What's Happening** is no one trusts the government. We know every president has **Different Strokes** once they get **In the House**. But **Gimme a Break**. Before you start expanding the government, you must reform it and make it functional. The government couldn't protect people from Bernard Madoff. The Securities and Exchange Commission couldn't protect us from Wall Street. If we are not careful, we are all going to end up in the **House of Payne**!

Sen. Reid Has A Lott To Learn From

Published: January 14, 2010

I n light of the recent revelation of Sen. Harry Reid's (D-NV) comments about President Obama's race, I feel compelled to try to add some sanity to the debate.

Sen. Reid is quoted as having said, "Obama could win the White House because he was a "light-skinned African-American with no Negro dialect, unless he wanted to have one."

This was a stupid comment, but not worthy of all the attention it is receiving. Does this mean Reid is a racist? Of course not. We must stop ignoring a public official's body of work just to score political points when the person makes an ill-advised comment. We all have said and done things we would not want the public to know about.

I have first hand experience with this type of situation. I helped former senator Trent Lott (R-MS) when he got caught up in a similar situation as Reid. Lott was and still is a good friend. Unlike Lott, Reid has the total support of the White House. But, Reid should be under no illusion, if they didn't need him to pass the president's health care bill, the support from some quarters of the administration might be different.

Reid is about to find out who his true friends are. I can assure you, that Lott has already reached out to Reid and given his unequivocal support and council. Lott can provide him with a great deal of insight on how to navigate this situation. Lott's resignation as majority leader had little to do with his comments about Strom Thurmond (R-SC) and everything to do with his political enemies seeing an opportunity to dethrone him as senate majority leader. Bush and Rove later lived to regret pulling the rug from underneath Lott.

What I find more disturbing than what Reid said or even Bill Clinton's comment about Obama getting him coffee is the feigned shock by those who have no public record of speaking out on racial issues. These people all of a sudden are filled with "unrighteous" indignation. People like Liz

Cheney (Dick Cheney's eldest daughter). I can find no record of her ever criticizing the people carrying signs calling President Obama "communist, fascist, Hitler," etc. She has never publically chastised Rush Limbaugh when he makes inflammatory remarks with racial overtones, nor the birthers, who claim Obama is not a U.S. citizen. With a name like Cheney, she has absolutely no standing to speak on anything racial, especially when it comes to Blacks.

If the issue is race, you can count on white, conservative front groups trotting out their favorite Blacks to attack liberals who cross the lines of race. Groups like Project 21 have trotted out people like Robert George, Mychal Massie, Bob Parks, Lisa Fritsch, and of course, no list would be complete without the obligatory addition of Ward CONnerly. He is a Black man that made his money off then governor of California, Pete Wilson's affirmative action programs. Then one day he was told to be against affirmative action and he just couldn't wait to get in front of a microphone. So, when white folks need a Black to trot out to speak against affirmative action, CONnerly is conditioned to volunteer without being called on.

When radical liberal groups like the NAACP, or the Congressional Black Caucus say that Lott's comment were racist and Reid's were not; what they mean is they agree with how Reid votes, therefore he can't be racist. I disagree with most things the Catholic Church stands for, but does that make me anti-Catholic? Why can't Lott disagree with Blacks on affirmative action, King's birthday, or certain government programs without being labeled a racist?

How many of you know that Lott was one of the main sponsors of a bill that allocated over a billion dollars to Black universities to update their technology infrastructure? Blacks must be more strategic and less emotional. Just because one disagrees with a person's voting record does not mean the person is a racist. This is part of the reason for the push back on a lot of racial issues by whites. They don't want to be vilified simply because they have a different view. Any fair minded person would agree. That's why dialogue is very important in matters like these.

I expected Michael Steele to call for Reid's resignation. As party chair, that's what he is supposed to do. But, I wish he and his director of coalitions, Angela Sailor, would be just as vocal criticizing those within and affiliated with the Republican Party. Sailor sent out an email this week detailing the democrat's hypocrisy in defending Reid. But she never sends out an email criticizing all the race-filled, hateful, insulting statements from Republicans who refuse to accept the fact that we have a duly elected Black president. Where is her email repudiating the vile comments Limbaugh made yesterday about Obama and the earthquake in Haiti? And they wonder why they can't get

Blacks to participate in the party (not that this is one of their goals).

For every Republican who makes a racially insensitive remark, I can find a Democrat who has done the same. So, after we have finished pointing fingers at each other, what have we accomplished? Absolutely nothing.

Reid and Lott are both good men. . I don't know Sen. Reid personally, but I will definitely go to war with and for Sen. Lott!

By all accounts, Reid and Lott are decent people and should be viewed through the totality of their lives. If the senator from Nevada's life were a book, I would consider it a good Reid!

Business As Usual

Published: February 18, 2010

C an you imagine Michael Jordan seeking advice on basketball from a ping pong player, or Tiger Woods seeking advice on his golf swing from a rugby player, or Bill Gates seeking advice on technology from a Buddhist monk?

Even Hollywood, with all its creative energy, could not have come up with such a script. Even if they did, no one would believe them. They would be run out of town. But, what would you say if I told you of a real life story that seems just as ridiculous, but yet, actually happened?

What if I told you the irony of all ironies was that it happened during Black History Month and there has been little public reaction to this amazing occurrence.

On February 10th, president Obama met with supposed "leaders" from the Black community to talk about the economy, how to create jobs, and the high unemployment rate within the Black community.

So far, so good. I don't think anyone would have an issue with that. As it is often stated, "when America sneezes, Black folks gets pneumonia." It is also well documented that during recessions, Black unemployment is always higher than the official number.

So, the president wanted to have an intimate, hour long meeting with 4 Black "leaders" that could shed some light on this problem. The invited participants were, Marc Morial, president of the National Urban League, Rev. Al Sharpton, president of the National Action Network, Benjamin Jealous, president of the NAACP and Dr. Dorothy I. Height, chairman, National Council of Negro Women (she was unable to make it due to the bad weather, she is 97).

I will give you a few minutes to stop laughing.

I find this to be an insult to every successful Black businessman and entrepreneur. What do these 4 people know about economics or job creation? How many jobs have they ever created, individually or collectively? Zero! Nada! Zilch!

I think Obama's presidency is about over if he is really seeking economic advice from people like these, whose policy agenda is antithetical to job creation (higher taxes, increased minimum wages, etc.).

Am I the only Black who is not only embarrassed by this, but also insulted by Obama's actions? If he was serious about dealing with these issues he would have met with Earvin "Magic" Johnson. Here's a former professional athlete who has proven you can make money by investing in the inner cities across America. He owns a chain of Starbucks, movie theaters, and restaurants all located in the inner city. Then there is Junior Bridgeman, retired N.B.A. player. He is president of Bridgeman Foods, Inc., which owns and operates Wendy's Hamburgers and other restaurants (103 Chili's) across the country. He is (and has been for many years) one of the largest Wendy's franchisees (over 160) in the world and is estimated to have revenues in the hundreds of millions dollars annually. David L. Steward, chairman & CEO, World Wide Technology of St. Louis, MO. He is the largest Black business in the U.S., with revenues in excess of $ 5 billion per year. The rapper Jay-Z (estimated to have a net worth upwards of $ 150 million). He owns a very successful fashion line and is part owner of the New Jersey Nets of the N.B.A. Then you have the usual cast of characters Obama should have met with,

Dick Parsons, chairman of Citigroup, Ken Chenault, CEO and chairman of American Express.

These are just a few of the people Obama should have been meeting with. What Obama did should be insulting to all Blacks. Let's be real. Obama had to do something to quiet the discontent from the radical liberals in the Democratic Party in general and Blacks specifically. This was his symbolic way of showing Blacks that he has not forgotten about us. He specially chose these individuals to meet with because they each have loud microphones plus he knew that would be happy with just a meeting. This cynical stunt buys the president some time to deal with other radical liberals who are giving him problems. He has silenced the gays by talking about "don't ask, don't tell." He's silenced the Hispanics by giving them Sonya Sotomayor to the U.S. Supreme Court. But, ironically, the biggest problem he has is the Democratic members of the House and Senate.

Obama knows that the Black folks he met with can do absolutely no harm to him politically. They can now go back to their groups and brag about being in the White House. They have already forgotten the fact that the president made no substantive commitments to them. Also unusual was the fact that the White House did not release any photos of the meeting, an indication of how unimportant they viewed the meeting.

Obama had no intention of having a serious discussion with these people about the economy and the Black community.   They wouldn't have understood the conversation even if the president did have sincere intentions.   What a cynical slap in the face to Blacks in general and Black business owners specifically.

Republicans are the Mecca of Hypocrisy

Published: August 5, 2010

Here we go again. We Republicans are supposed to be the party of the rule of law, smaller government, and individual freedom. But every time I turn around, I am confused by the hypocrisy our party will display for political expediency.

The most glaring example of this in recent time was the case of Terri Schiavo back in 2005. She became brain dead due to an accident and her husband wanted to remove her from all life support. Her family asked Republicans to usurp the authority of her husband by way of various political maneuvers to strip the husband of his right to make medical decisions about his wife. Ultimately the federal courts sided with the husband and she was removed from life support.

Republicans were more interested in scoring political points than protecting the rights of an individual not to have the government interfere in the private affairs of a spouse. Whether you agreed with the husband's decision or not was totally irrelevant. This was one of the reasons Republicans lost control of congress in 2006.

Now, they are repeating the same mistake in 2010 in the case of the proposed mosque near the site of the twin towers in New York that were destroyed during the attacks on 9/11.

Two days ago, The Landmarks Preservation Commission of New York City voted 9-0 to reject landmark status for the building that is on the site of the proposed mosque. If the commission had granted landmark status, the building could not have been torn down, thus killing the project.

The decision paves the way for construction of the project to begin. The project is to include a mosque and an Islamic community center. The project is being spear-headed by a group called the Cordoba Initiative. According to them, they are a group of moderate Muslims. The total project cost is approximately $ 100 million (raised by private money). So, what is controversial about this? Absolutely nothing.

Republicans have decided to play politics and play on religious intolerance to score political points. But, as in the Schiavo case, this too will backfire. Now, I will give you the stated reason why opponents are against this project. I hope you are seated—with seatbelt on. Their opposition is based on the great "legal" principle that the "location would be insensitive (because the group is Muslim) and it disrespects the memory of 9/11 victims." Yes, you heard me right—**INSENSITIVE**. They claim the site is too close to the twin towers that were destroyed on 9/11.

Now, I will tell you who "they" are. Some of the most notable opponents of the project are: 9/11 first-responders, family members of those killed in the attack, former New York congressman and current Republican gubernatorial candidate, Rick Lazio, Abraham Foxman from the Anti-Defamation League, former speaker of the house, Newt Gingrich, Sarah Palin, radio entertainers, Rush Limbaugh and Laura Ingraham, to name a few.

These are all people that are supposed to be big supporters of the first amendment (freedom of speech) and the right of the individual and the rule of law. But yet, they supported the attempted hijacking of a government body in their attempts to strip away the rights of Muslim Americans to erect a building.

Is this what Republicans mean when they talk about "limited government?" Government that is limited only to what they believe?

After the vote to allow the buildings to go up, Foxman arrogantly stated, "the group's proposal fail to address the crux of opponents' criticism that erecting the mosque near ground zero is insensitive to 9/11 victims' families." Foxman continues, "Some legitimate questions have been raised about the Cordoba Initiative's funding and possible ties with groups whose ideologies stand in contradiction to our shared values."

Has he lost his mind? So, he believes in individual freedom as long as it's agreeable to him? This issue is not about terrorism or Muslims, or 9/11. This is about the rule of law—I thought a core bedrock Republican principle.

These are the same Republicans who want Obama to enforce our immigration laws, but don't want New York City to enforce the laws that give these Muslim Americans the right to build their Islamic community center near ground zero!

To the family members of those killed during 9/11, your personal pain should not be used to deny an American citizen the exercise of his constitutional rights. Would you feel the same way if the Catholic Church was erecting the building?

This whole debate has an undercurrent of religious intolerance. Politicians and talk radio are trying to push specific agendas at the expense of individual liberty and freedom. Did Republicans learn nothing from the Terri Schiavo disaster?

Maybe we should build a shrine to the Republican Party at ground zero and call it the "Mecca of Hypocrisy."

The Flag of Hypocrisy

Published: August 19, 2010

I am amazed that the controversy surrounding the proposed Muslim mosque and community center in New York City at ground zero is still going strong. America has turned into a country where if you don't agree with someone, you are painted as a bad person. This is exactly what is going on in New York City.

Those who oppose the project have lost the legal battle, but now they are attempting to turn it into a political battle. I find those in opposition full of hypocrisy, especially those in the Republican Party.

When President Obama used the word "empathy" to describe one of the qualities he looked for in a Supreme Court nominee, Republicans ripped into him (and rightfully so). Our legal system is based on the law, not how one feels about a given case or person involved in a case.

Now, when it comes to the proposed mosque at ground zero, these same people want the Muslim community to be "sensitive" (i.e. empathetic) towards the family members of those killed and others impacted my 9/11. Mind you that everyone agrees that the Muslims have the legal right to move forward with the project—not even the most vocal opponent argues this point.

Their whole argument is about "sensitivity." How ironic that when Obama suggested empathy in a Supreme Court nominee, he was excoriated. Now, these very same people are encouraging the same thing, albeit in a different circumstance.

As a longtime Republican, I have had many conversations with white folks in the party regarding the confederate flag (pictured above) and its place in our society. These people see absolutely no problem with the flag flying on the dome of state capitols around the country, even though they know it's very offensive to the Black community.

I have been told on many occasions that I (and the Black community) was being overly sensitive and that those who support the flying of the flag are within their rights. Additionally, I was told, you can't expect people to forget their heritage because of the sensitivities of the Black community. After all, "me nor my parents or grandparents were part of the confederacy. But, it is party of our family's history; therefore, we celebrate it. We had nothing to do with slavery, nor do we support any type of discrimination."

Isn't this the same argument the Muslims are using in New York? They had nothing to do with 9/11. But, yet they want to be able to celebrate their religion, despite the bad feelings that others may experience.

Once again, these same Republicans who oppose the Muslims in New York on grounds of "sensitivity," will not take the same stand on the confederate flag when it comes to the Black community. Principles are guides to one's life that are not relative or situational. Principles have to be consistently applied for one to be credible and maintain the moral high ground. You can't pick and choose when to apply one's principles.

Through what's going on in New York, maybe, just maybe, Republicans will better understand how Blacks feel about the confederate flag. And maybe, just maybe, the next time Blacks express their feelings about having the confederate flag flying atop government buildings, Republicans won't just blow us off. But, maybe they will be "sensitive" to the pain the flag evokes within our community.

Can you honor the confederate flag without being a racist? Without a doubt. Can you support the Muslim project in New York without being "insensitive?" Without a question.

To believe one without the other is to fly the flag of hypocrisy.

Jim Clyburn-ed

Published: November 18, 2010

I n the immortal words of civil rights legend, Fannie Lou Hamer, when will Blacks become "sick and tired of being sick and tired?"

Once again the Democratic Party has shown its disdain for the Black community and Black Democrats, as usual, just sit back and continue to allow it to happen.

Blacks vote Democratic upwards of 92% during presidential elections and about 90 % during congressional elections. Can Blacks actually say they have received a sufficient return on their investment for that level of support? Of course not. So, why do Blacks continue to allow Democrats to marginalize and disrespect them?

Jim Clyburn, Congressman from South Carolina and current Majority Whip in the House of Representatives (making him the 3rd highest ranking person in the Democratic Party) was seeking reelection to his leadership post until he was forced to withdraw last Saturday night.

In the House, the leadership positions are: Speaker of the House (Nancy Pelosi), Majority Leader (Steny Hoyer), and Majority Whip (Jim Clyburn).

Since the Democrats lost the elections, they have become the minority party, thus will lose the Majority Leader position. As opposed to finding a new leadership position in the minority, Hoyer decided to challenge Clyburn for this position.

Not one word of protest from the first Black president of the U.S. Not one word from the first female Speaker of the House. Not one word from Hispanic members of Congress who constantly want Blacks to support their bids for amnesty for their people.

On Saturday night Clyburn was forced to withdraw from his bid to become Minority Whip so that Hoyer could assume the same position. In exchange, Pelosi created a "new" leadership position so that Clyburn could have a position at the leadership table.

Are you kidding me?

Why is it that the Democrats always ask the Black candidate to back out of a race and not the white candidate? This is the same party that makes a regular point about how "racist" the Republican Party is supposed to be.

Why didn't Pelosi force Hoyer to drop out of the race? She could have created a "new" leadership position for him. This is the same party that, in September, tried to force current Congressman from Florida, Kendrick Meek, to drop out of his race to become the first Black elected U.S. senator from Florida. The White House asked Bill Clinton to pressure Meek to withdraw from the race and support the governor of Florida, Charlie Crist. Mind you that Crist is a white Republican turned Independent. Meek resisted the pressure and said no.

So, the Democrats care so much for the Black community that they wanted Meek to drop out of the race and endorse a de facto Republican. Again, where were the voices of the most loyal voting block within the Democratic Party?

What makes me most angry is the total silence of those in the Black community. Clyburn has spent 4 years as Majority Whip. During this time, Clyburn has done favors for many Democratic groups that have come to him for help. Where were the voices of outrage from these groups? Why didn't they promise holy hell if the Democrats didn't keep Clyburn in his leadership position?

Where was Marc Morial (head of the National Urban League)? Where was Al Sharpton (head of the National Action Network)? Where was Ben Jealous (head of the N.A.A.C.P.)? Where were groups like the National Medical Association (Black doctors), National Council of Negro Women, Leadership Council on Civil Rights, National Newspapers Publishers of America (Black newspapers), The National Coalition on Black Civic Participation, The National Association of Black Accountants, The National Black M.B.A.s, NAFEO, or all the Black Universities?

I will let you in on a little secret. The reason why the Democrats continue to insult the Black community is because we allow them to. Democrats fear no retribution from Blacks. Obama has met with the Hispanic Caucus on several occasions to discuss amnesty for illegals. How many times has he met with the Black Caucus? Maybe 1 time! Obama fears the Hispanic community (and their votes); but has absolutely no fear of losing the Black vote; therefore, he felt no need to intervene in Clyburn's race or any other issue of particular concern to the Black community.

To my Republican friends, this is a classic case for the value of diversity. Clyburn and Hoyer are both equally qualified for the position of Minority Whip. So, if all other things are equal, you have to give the nod to diversity, lest you have an all-white leadership team!

Everyone knows that I am a Republican. But, why is it that I seem more upset and insulted by the actions of the Democratic Party, than Black Democrats?

Clyburn is a very decent man and a great political strategist. I know he has been helpful to all of the above groups and individuals. He has extended himself tirelessly to help with their causes. But, yet none of these groups came to his defense.

Blacks should have made it clear to Obama, Pelosi and Hoyer, that there would be hell to pay if Clyburn was challenged. Blacks are the most loyal voting block in the Democratic Party and they have nothing to show for it.

When all is said and done, there's more said than done.

Israel's Thoughts About Black Group Is Real

Published: March 17, 2011

O nce again Black Democrats have been dissed by the Democratic leadership in the U.S. House of Representatives; and once again there was absolutely no price to pay.

When will Blacks finally, in the immortal words of civil rights pioneer, Fannie Lou Hamer, get "sick and tired of being sick and tired?" Democrats continue to treat Blacks like second class citizens because no one fears any retaliation or any consequence for how they treat Blacks.

Even the first Black president of the U.S., Barack Obama, has learned that lesson early on. Mind you, it took him almost a year and a half before he finally met with the Congressional Black Caucus (CBC). But yet in his first year, he met with Latinos (about amnesty for illegals), gays (about recognizing gay marriage, etc.).

Obama, like Congressman Steve Israel, knows that Blacks will only complain about being mistreated for a day or so and then accept the most meager of apologies in order to move beyond whatever slight.

This leads me to what Israel said in a meeting with members of the Congressional Black Caucus last week.

Congressman Steve Israel (D-NY) chairs the Democratic Congressional Campaign Committee (DCCC--he is responsible for getting Democratic House members reelected or elected). Israel attended the CBC's weekly luncheon last week and was quoted by members in attendance as having said, "Can we win the House without the CBC? Yes. Do we want to win the House without the CBC? No." Israel all but admitted that the quote is accurate.

As usual, the CBC got all worked up and huffed and puffed until Israel agreed to meet with them again the following day to work through their hurt feelings.

So, what was the result of the follow up meeting? Drum roll please----Israel and CBC Chairman Emanuel Cleaver (D—MO) issued a joint statement saying their meeting was "constructive" and announced that Assistant Leader Jim

Clyburn (D-SC) would chair a new Member Advisory Board at the DCCC.

This is the same highly respected Clyburn who was forced out of leadership after the Democrats lost the elections in November—and the CBC stood by and watched him be pushed out of his leadership position (see my column from last November regarding this issue).

So, how many times will members of the CBC allow their party leaders to shame and embarrass them before they take a principled stand that has measureable consequences?

Blacks are the most loyal voting block in the Democratic Party, but they have yet to get anything approaching a sufficient return on their investment for their loyalty. This has little to do with race and more to do with raw political power.

If Blacks are going to continue to blindly give their loyalty to the Democrats and not demand anything in return—why would the party give them anything?

Too often Blacks get angry when they should be getting even. I challenge my readers to name one specific thing Obama or the Democrats have done that was uniquely to the benefit of Blacks? I can name a whole list of things geared towards the gay, Latino, Jewish, union communities, etc.

In a rare moment of candor and honesty, Israel said publically what everyone has been saying privately for many years—the Black community never demands anything for their vote; they just want to be made to feel good with symbolic gestures.

They want things like, visiting their churches or singing "We Shall Overcome," or taking a picture with them.

In many ways, being a Black Democrat is like being a Black Republican—it's kind of like peeing on yourself in a dark blue suit; it gives you a warm feeling, but no one ever notices!

I don't have a problem with what Israel said to the CBC. He was speaking the truth. Furthermore, if the CBC is so upset about what he said, then what are they prepared to do about it other than agree to be part of a meaningless advisory board?

Israel was not being insensitive or racist with his comments. What Israel said is real.

A Bad Joint

Published: August 4, 2011

The Joint Center for Political and Economic Studies used to be one of the preeminent think tanks in Washington, DC. They focus on issues of particular concern to the Black community.

Over the years I have participated in or hosted panels with them that were very substantive and informative. They were a think tank in its truest form---there to provide unbiased analysis, not to promote and agenda!

Unfortunately, those days are gone. They no longer have the standing that they once had. As a matter of fact, they have almost become invisible to the public at large because they have lost their vision.

I learned this from my personal experience with them this past Monday.

On Monday, the U.S. House of Representatives passed a bill that increased the U.S. debt limit (the U.S. Senate did the same on Tuesday). So, that afternoon I received an email from the Joint Center about them hosting a webinar to discuss the vote on increasing the debt ceiling and its impact on "vulnerable populations." The full title was, "The Debt and Deficit Debate and the Untold Story of the Impact on Vulnerable Populations."

They never identified or defined what was a "vulnerable population."

According to their press release, "The Joint Center for Political and Economic Studies has scheduled a webinar today to focus on the challenges facing African Americans and other people of color, and particularly their concerns that measures related to the debt ceiling debate could exacerbate already high unemployment and undermine short-term and long-term economic prospects.

Journalists who dial in will have the opportunity to question members of two panels – the first of which will be comprised of a member of the **Congressional Black Caucus, the White House National Economic Council** and leading national economists and will examine the details and projected impact of the negotiated agreement that Congress will vote on. The second panel will delve further into the agreement's program reductions on members of vulnerable populations and on both discretionary and entitlement programs that they rely upon."

As if the above wasn't bad enough, I was totally incensed when I saw the list of their panelists:

Ralph B. Everett, Esq., President and CEO Joint Center for Political and Economic Studies, Avis Jones-DeWeever, Ph.D., Executive Director National Council of Negro Women, The Honorable Bobby Scott (D-VA) U.S. House of Representatives, and a member of the White House's National Economic Council (this is just a partial listing, for the complete list go to:

http://www.jointcenter.org/newsroom/press-releases/americas-fiscal-crisis-and-the-untold-story-of-the-impact-on-vulnerable-popu).

During the webinar I sent a complaint to the person running the session and she indicated that she would have someone call me after the event to discuss my complaint that the panel was bias and comprised of all Democrats.

So, the next morning, Gina Wood (the Director of Policy and Planning) called me and I expressed my concerns to her. She became extremely defensive, rude, and was very arrogant. These are common traits of radical feminists like her. They have no intellectual capital to rely on, so they get emotional and rude.

When I expressed my disappointment that every panelist was a Democrat, she said, "I had no knowledge of the panelists politics....I reviewed some of their writings and used that as the basis of my inviting them to be on the panel." So, I responded by asking her did she honestly believe that I was stupid enough to think that she didn't know that Bobby Scott was a liberal Democratic member of Congress? It went downhill from there. I had to terminate the phone call with extreme rectitude with malice aforethought (in other words, I hung up on the girl).

I am not going to have someone pee on me and then try to make me believe it's raining. The Joint Center is better than that. I can't believe they would actually have a panel totally devoted to White House talking points and yet, claim to be nonpartisan. When I challenged Gina on that point, she had no response. She knows very well that for them to have integrity, they must present more than one view in order to have a real discussion. But they are not nonpartisan. They are an extension of the Democratic National Committee (DNC).

The Joint Center can no longer be taken seriously if they cannot be honest with themselves and the American people. Either they are going to provide a forum for spirited discussions of issues of concern to the Black community or they are going to continue to be an arm of the DNC. Either way is fine with me, but can we have a little "truth in advertising."

If Gina Wood is representative of the Joint Center's integrity, then their reputations is going to go up in smoke!

The Plane Truth

Published: December 15, 2011

How many of you fly on airplanes or frequent government buildings? If you do, you know you must show some type of government I.D. to get on a plane or enter into a government building.

To my knowledge, I have never heard anyone claim they were discriminated against if they were not allowed to fly or enter a government building because they didn't have an I.D. To the contrary, people know the rules in advance, so therefore they comply.

I don't know anyone (young or old, Black or white) who doesn't have any form of government sanctioned I.D. (driver's license, passport, etc.).

Even grandma, who is retired and needs to cash her check, has some form of government I.D.

I think most of us can agree that it is a good thing to make people provide "legitimate" I.D. before getting on a plane or entering into a government building, or cashing a check.

I don't think many people would consider this an intrusion or inconvenience. There is a safety component to this requirement that helps protect everyone.

So, to ensure the safety of the general public, the government has mandated these requirements in order to participate in certain activities.

So, can one argue that if one doesn't have these forms of government I.D. that they have been discriminated against? Secondly, if one doesn't have any form of I.D., should the government be obligated to pay the cost to get them?

Again, I challenge my readers to identify one person that they know personally that doesn't have some form of government I.D.

If you agree with me that the government's requirement that one have "legitimate" government I.D. to get on a plane or into a government building; how can you then argue that to require the same in order to vote in political elections is discriminatory against the poor and minorities?

Poor people fly on airplanes and enter into government buildings like everyone else. These are the absurd arguments being made by the radical liberals like Al Sharpton, Ben Jealous, and radical liberal organizations like the N.A.A.C.P., the Congressional Black Caucus, etc.

If it's racist to require I.D. for people to vote, then it must be racist to require I.D. to board a plane or enter a government building!

Liberals never want to match a government program with any type of individual responsibility. They constantly argue the extreme. They claim minorities are adversely affected by requiring I.D. in order to vote. According to them, the poor can't afford the cost to pay for proper I.D. They argue that grandma doesn't have her original birth certificate; therefore it is much harder for her to get her I.D.

If the laws only applied to minorities or the poor, then I would agree with the liberals; but the law applies equally to rich and poor, Black and white.

Why do liberals constantly argue that if something is difficult or that you are required to actually do something in order to get a benefit, it somehow is discriminatory?

Again, I challenge my readers to name me one person they know personally who doesn't have a government I.D.

Those who may not have a government I.D. are statistically negligible. So, to make policy based on the exception is crazy. It is not difficult to get a government I.D. and to argue differently is simply not the plain truth.

Blacks Schooled to Stay in a Daze

Published: May 29, 2013

L ast week I was flipping through the TV channels and came across one of Spike Lee's best movies, School Daze. This was a 1988 film written and directed by Lee. The movie took an inside look at some of the internal issues that go on within the Black community—issues like dark skinned Blacks versus light skinned Blacks; Blacks that have "good" hair versus Blacks with "nappy" hair; Blacks from wealthy families versus Blacks from poor families. The movie was funny and serious at the same time. I always say that comedy is simply a funny way of being serious.

The movie's setting takes place on the fictional Black college campus of Mission College. Lee's concept for the movie was based on his experiences he had as a student at

Morehouse College, as well as his interactions with students from Spelman College and Clark Atlanta University. These schools are predominately occupied by children of the Black elite. They are all located in Atlanta, GA.

The movie received critical acclaim and was a financial success.

The movie created a firestorm of controversy because the elite Blacks did not take well to criticism of their disdain of Blacks who were not part of their clique—just ask Bill Cosby.

Though the school in the movie was named Mission College, it was actually shot on the campuses of Morehouse, Spelman and Clark Atlanta. But, because of the movie's portrayal of the Black bourgeoisie, Lee was forced to stop filming on those campuses and was barred from being invited to speak on their campuses after the movie was released. He was forced to complete his filming at nearby Morris Brown College, a lesser known Black college that was not known to have many people from wealthy backgrounds.

Not much has changed in the 25 years since the release of School Daze. As a matter of fact, one could argue that this schism within the Black community has gotten worse.

This view is personified in the person of President Barak Obama. He is light skinned, has no connection with the Black community, Ivy League educated, and seems very uncomfortable around Blacks who are not part of the bourgeoisie.

He is more comfortable talking about Newtown than he is Chi-town (Chicago). He hangs with the likes of Jay-Z, Beyoncé, Alicia Keys, and Hill Harper to give him "street cred."

But yet he ignores the very issues that gave birth to the Hip-Hop nation—police brutality, Black on Black crime, teenage pregnancy, the glorification of the drug culture, etc.

The Blacks that have regular access to this White House rarely, if ever, lift their voices to address some of the needs and concerns of those who can't afford to raise thousands of dollars for the president.

These Blacks have not once criticized the Obama administration's lack of action in regards to the issues of particular concern to the Black community. Oh, I forgot, they don't want to jeopardize their invitations to the White House's Christmas party.

These Blacks rationalize that Obama can't afford to be seen doing anything specifically for Blacks for fear that Obama will be called a Black president. Well, I thought he was the first Black president?

So, let me make sure I understand this; it's ok to do specific things for the Black bourgeoisie—private invitations to the White House, rides on Air Force One, private movie screenings at the White House-but he can't do things specifically to address the high unemployment rate in the Black community?

Lee's movie has quite an emotional, but yet powerful ending. Laurence Fishburne, one of the main actors in the movie, awakens from his sleep (along with the rest of the cast) and meets in the middle of the campus with his pajamas on. Then he screams several times at the top of his voice, "W-A-K-E UP."

Unfortunately, under Obama, the Black bourgeoisie have yet to wake up.

The Republican Party Needs A Cadillac

Published: February 16, 2012

Recently, I had lunch with a very powerful Republican elected official who is a good friend of mine. We have extremely candid conversations; especially about race (he is white). Out of nowhere he asked me what was the reason Blacks have a historical affinity for Cadillac automobiles (named after the French explorer who founded Detroit in 1701).

I responded by saying the same reason Blacks had a historical affinity for the Republican Party. He looked very confused and said, "What does that have to do with my question?"

I then said to him, "Let me teach you a little history."

The Republican Party was founded with the express purpose of ending the slavery of Blacks. Blacks remained loyal to the Republican Party until the party made the decision to adopt the "Southern strategy."

The Southern strategy was implemented by Nixon aide, Kevin Phillips in the 1960s. The strategy drove a wedge between the Black community and the Republican Party. The party increasingly became hostile to civil rights in order to get white, Southern Democrats to join the Republican Party. It has worked magnificently ever since, with Blacks voting Republican only 10% on average during a presidential election.

Cadillac had a similar strategy by not selling their cars to Blacks.

Most people are familiar with the name Cadillac (made by General Motors). But, most are unfamiliar with the story of how Cadillac almost went out of business during the depression (1928-1934) because of their prejudice towards Blacks.

Likewise, the modern day Republican Party is in great danger of going down the same road as the Cadillac, but with a much different result—they will go out of business.

Republicans can no longer afford to be the all-white Southern male party. They can no longer afford to totally ignore and disregard the Black community. They can no longer afford to have all whites at the decision making table. Some will say, yes they can. Let's get back to Cadillac.

Nicolas Dreystadt singlehandedly saved Cadillac from their own ignorance. He was a German immigrant who came to the U.S. with his parents when he was a small boy. He worked as a mechanic apprentice for Mercedes-Benz before becoming the national head of Cadillac's services department. He was responsible for the department that serviced Cadillac cars throughout the U.S. He was considered middle-management.

As he travelled across the U.S. to monitor Cadillac's service departments, Dreystadt noticed something strange. He noticed great numbers of Blacks bringing their cars in to be serviced. "But how could this be," he thought, knowing that Cadillac had a strict "no sale to Blacks" policy. Then it dawned on him that these Blacks had paid a white to buy the cars for them and they paid a fee for the transaction.

"But the wealthy Negro," business critic Peter F. Drucker recalled, "wanted a Cadillac so badly that he paid a substantial premium to a white man to front for him in buying one. Dreystadt had investigated this unexpected phenomenon and found that a Cadillac was the only success symbol the affluent black could buy; he had no access to good housing, to luxury resorts, or to any other of the outward signs of worldly success (Cadillacs cost more than $ 5,000 back then-- over $ 60,000 in today's money)."

The last straw for Dreystadt was when he found out that Cadillac would not allow boxing champion Joe Louis to buy a car, but that he paid a white person to buy it for him. Lewis war revered as an icon by both whites and Blacks.

So, in 1932, Dreystadt did the unthinkable. General Motor's Chairman, Alfred P. Sloan had called a board meeting to discuss closing down the Cadillac line of cars because of low sales due to the depression. Dreystadt just happened to be in Detroit at the same time. So, unannounced he asked the board for 10 minutes to discuss his plan for saving Cadillac.

One person described Dreystadt's actions as akin to someone knocking on the door to the Vatican asking the College of Cardinals for 10 minutes while they are in the middle of electing a Pope.

Dreystadt pointed out that blacks paid a premium to white buyers to front for them. "Why should a bunch of white front men get several hundred dollars each when that profit could flow to General Motors? Demand like this should be exploited. Dreystadt urged the executive committee to go after this market. The board bought his reasoning and gave him 18 months to develop the "Negro" market. By the end of 1934, Cadillac sales increased by 70%, and the division actually broke even. Dreystadt was eventually made head of the Cadillac Division.

The definitive book on Dreystadt is, "The Chrome Colossus", by Ed Cray. According to Cray, "Overwhelmed by Dreystadt's audacity and bemused by his proposal, the committee gave him eighteen months in which to develop the Negro market. By the end of 1934, Derystadt had the Cadillac division breaking even, and by 1940 had multiplied sales tenfold…It was for business reasons that the Cadillac division of General Motors began marketing to blacks. In the 1920s, Cadillac sold to whites only, to maintain an exclusive image. When the Depression hit, the division was on the ropes, and executive Nicholas Dreystadt realized the black elite-singers, boxers, doctors, and lawyers had been paying white front-men to buy their Cadillacs. Dreystadt decided that selling to black Americans was good business."

Allow me to digress. Dreystadt did another unthinkable thing during this same time period according to Crane. "Dreystadt had accepted a contract to produce delicate aircraft gyroscopes. Despite mutterings on the fourteenth floor that the job was a killer and needed skilled hands unavailable. The dissent turned to outrage when Dreystadt and his personnel manager, Jim Roche, hired 2,000 average black prostitutes from Paradise Valley–uneducated, untrained, but willing workers.

Dreystadt hired the madams too, blithely explaining, "They know how to manage the women…Within weeks the women were surpassing quotas, and the outrage turned to chagrin on West Grand Boulevard. Jokes about Cadillac's "red-light district" angered Dreystadt. These women are my fellow workers, and yours, he insisted. They do a good job and respect their work.

Whatever their past, they are entitled to the same respect as any one of our associates…Dreystadt knew he would have to replace these women at war's end–returning veterans had job preference, and the United Auto Workers, heavily white male with a southern-states orientation, wanted the women out of the plant.

"Nigger-lover" and "whore-monger" Dreystadt fought to keep some, pleading, "For the first time in their lives, these poor wretches are paid decently, work in decent conditions, and have some rights. And for the first time they have some dignity and self-respect. It's our duty to save them from being again rejected and despised." The union stood adamant.

When the women were laid off, a number committed suicide rather than return to the streets. Nick Dreystadt grieved, "God forgive me. I have failed these poor souls."

So, to my Republican Party, when will you to realize that marketing to Black voters "is good business?" Just like Blacks saved Cadillac, Blacks can also save the Republican Party.

But, unlike the executives of Cadillac, when the Republican "Nicholas Dreystadt" knocked on the door and wanted to discuss how to market your party to the Black community, you refused to listen. That person was the late former

Congressman Jack Kemp. He, like Dreystadt, understood the value of the Black vote and preached to anyone who would listen.

Cadillac was wrong for refusing to sell their product to the Black community, but at least they had sense enough to set aside their prejudice when the choice was between Blacks and nonexistence.

You have no Blacks on staff at the Republican National Committee (or any of its other committees), there are no Blacks on staff of any of the presidential campaigns. Republicans like myself and former Congressman J.C. Watts have repeatedly tried to be the modern day Dreystadt, but maybe after a few more electoral loses you will awaken to the most loyal customer you have ever had.

New Gun Legislation Is Not The Answer

Published: January 17, 2013

Wisdom is the principle thing, therefore get wisdom; but with all they getting, get understanding (Proverbs 4:7).

I really had not planned on writing anything about the shooting in Newtown, CT because I didn't have anything fresh or thought provoking to write. As I have previously written, it's hard for me to get worked up about Connecticut, when young kids are dying every day in Chicago and they barely get a mention in the news, and definitely not by this White House.

The worst thing any politician can ever do is to legislate in a cloud of emotion. Every time Americans have a tragedy, politicians and the public demand that "something" be done to prevent the same event from happening again. I am reminded of the old expression, "hindsight is 20/20."

Let me say as emphatically as possible, there is no current law or future law that can prevent another mass shooting from occurring. Guns are not the problem, it's the people. If we could magically ban all guns immediately, it will have absolutely no impact on violent crime. There are an estimated 300 million guns in the hands of Americans. So, if guns are banned prospectively, what are you going to do about the guns already in the hands of Americans?

These liberals who want to take the 300 million guns away from law abiding citizens are the same ones who say it is impossible to find and remove 12 million illegals from this country. Is it really easier to find guns than it is humans? But I digress.

I am not taking a position either way on the issue of gun control, but I do think there should be some sanity brought into the discussion. The National Rifle Association (NRA) really needs to shut its mouth. They are coming across as so unreasonable and they continue to embarrass themselves with every press release or statement they utter.

Liberals, including those in the White House, don't want to talk about the moral issues necessary to deal with all this violence. Children are growing up in single parent households, babies are having babies, Johnnie has two daddies, and Susie has two mommies. We have quickly become a nation with no standards or any absolutes.

When I grew up, there was male and female. Now there is this notion of "sexual fluidity." This is a growing notion that is sweeping across the country indicating that your sexual preferences are constantly changing—thus is fluid. So, a male sometimes wants to be with a woman, sometimes he wants to be with a man, and sometimes he wants to be with both simultaneously.

We have a society that obsesses about their rights, but never mentions their responsibilities. Christians, especially preachers, are apologizing for their beliefs all in the guise of wanting to be liked.

Well, you can pass all the gun control laws you want, but until you deal with the heart of a man and the culture of a society, there can be no peace. Everyone knows that killing is wrong, but yet we subject people to literally thousands of hours of the most violent images from cradle to grave; and then we wonder why someone goes into a movie theater and shoots total strangers.

You have preachers apologizing for speaking against the homosexual lifestyle and some even remaining silent because they don't want to hurt people's feelings. Parents are telling their children that they are at fault when their own kid punches them in the face because they took away their cell phone.

There is wrong and right; there are winners and losers. Mass shootings in Connecticut, Colorado or Virginia are not about gun control, but rather values. Liberal Hollywood puts out all kinds of violent, over the top sexually charged programs; but says it's just entertainment.

The NRA sees no circumstance by which they are willing to compromise on their right to bear arms, not even for the good of the country. Let not your good be evil spoken of. This whole notion of universal background checks, while optically and from a PR perspective seems very reasonable; will do nothing to prevent another mass shooting.

Criminals don't buy guns, they still guns. So, requiring background checks will prevent a very negligible few from obtaining guns, but 99% of gun purchasers are law abiding citizens with no mental health issues.

So, making people submit to background checks may make society feel good, but it doesn't address the problem.

Having the minister pray for your speedy recovery after surgery will make you feel good, but you still better take that pain medication in conjunction with that prayer.

So, to the politicians, legislate if you must. But until you deal with the issue of values, you have become as the sounding brass or the tingling cymbal, full of sound and fury, signifying nothing.

An Apology to Jesse Jackson

Published: March 6, 2013

Those who know me know that I will be the first to admit that I am not always right; but I am never wrong. So, after many years of being a columnist, I am compelled to utter the words that I never dreamed I would ever have to say—I was wrong!

I did a column in 2008 titled, **"Winners and Losers from Election '08."** I listed Jesse Jackson, Sr. as one of the biggest losers of that year. Here is what I said, "His past contributions to America are undeniable, but his future place is uncertain. Every time he opened his mouth in the past year, he said something negative about Obama. First, Jackson criticized Obama for "acting white" because he was not as forceful as Jesse wanted regarding the Jena 6 case in Louisiana. Then there was the infamous Fox News open mic incident where Jackson is heard saying, "See, Barack has been talking down to Black people…telling niggers how to behave…I wanna cut his nuts out." Finally, in October Jackson was speaking at the first World Policy Forum in Evian, France. Published reports have him saying if Obama is elected as president, "fundamental changes in U.S. foreign policy" will occur.

He said the most important change would occur in the Middle East, where "decades of putting Israel's interests first" would end. Jackson's reputation has been forever tarnished.

Jesse accused Obama of "acting white" in response to Obama's tepid response to the Jena Six. The Jena Six were 6 Black juvenile high school students in Jena, Louisiana who were arrested and charged with attempted second-degree murder for the beating of a fellow white student. The charges were later reduced to aggravated second-degree battery and conspiracy. Many believed the prosecutor filed the more serious charges because the accused juveniles were Black. As we all know, Obama has no history of taking strong positions on anything when it involves Blacks.

Jesse got it right when he accused Obama of "talking down to Black people." Everyone, including myself, eviscerated him for making the comment and accused him of being jealous of Obama. How can we forget when Obama spoke at the Congressional Black Caucus dinner a couple years ago and told Blacks to "stop complaining?" Jesse saw something in Obama that the rest of us missed and now we are paying the price for it, especially Blacks.

Jackson was right on point with his prediction about the changing U.S. relations with the Middle East. Our relationship with Israel has never been more volatile than it is now.

In my view, the Black community specifically and America in general wanted so badly to show the world that, in 2008, our country could be held up as the model for true democracy and equality. America wanted to prove that anyone, regardless of background, who played by the rules and had a vision, could be president of the United States.

To his credit, Jesse saw beyond the rhetoric and somehow had the ability to see deep inside of Obama's soul; thus trying to warn us of what we were getting. So, again, to Jesse Jackson, I was wrong and you were spot on. You saw a level of arrogance and detachment from the Black community that most of us were blinded to. You knew he would not pay attention to the high unemployment rate in the Black community. You knew he would not spend political capital on the high murder rate in Chicago. You knew he would continue to talk down to Black people.

You were rightly ostracized for your comments back in 2008, but on this issue of Obama's disdain for Blacks; you must be embraced and brought back into the fold. When I was a child, I spoke as a child, I thought as a child; but when I became a man, I put those childish things behind me.

We wanted Obama to win on many levels, but Jesse has taught us that we should never allow emotions to cloud our judgment. I'm not always right, but I am rarely wrong.

Like Cholesterol, Some Discrimination Is Good

Published: May 2, 2013

Last week I was on Washington Watch with Roland Martin. This is a weekly TV show that deals with political issues relative to the Black community. The roundtable discussion was very lively, but I was amazed at my fellow panelist's response to something I said.

Americans somehow has this strange notion that all discrimination is bad. But it isn't. We discriminate everyday. You choose one restaurant over another; you watch one TV show versus another; you date skinny girls and not heavy girls.

As a matter of fact, some discrimination is quite healthy. If you know drug dealers sell their drugs in certain neighborhoods, why would you go there if you have no interest in buying drugs? If you are allergic to smoke, why would you go to a bar that allows smoking? If certain countries are more likely to kidnap an American tourist, why would you go there if you are an American?

I think most reasonable people would agree that this type of discrimination is good and healthy. Similarly, our immigration policy should have a certain level of discrimination built into the policy. I was totally surprised that my fellow panelists disagreed. They seemed to be in favor of an open borders approach to immigration. The open borders crowd basically believes that anyone who wants to come to America has a right to come here if they follow the rules.

I find this view very idiotic. If you are not an American citizen, then you have absolutely no basis for the assertion of any right. Post 911, at a minimum, our immigration policy should discriminate based on country of origin.

We know that certain countries are a hotbed for producing terrorist: Saudi Arabia, Yemen, Somalia, Chechnya, etc. So, why would our immigration policy even allow people from those countries to come to the U.S. for any reason, let alone to get a green card or citizenship?

Is this discrimination? You damn right—it's the good kind of discrimination. You don't see terrorists being trained in Australia, the Seychelles, or Trinidad & Tobago, so therefore there should be less concern about immigrants from these countries. Is this not reasonable?

American visas, green cards and citizenship are not rights, but are privileges. No one has a right to enter into our country and we don't need to justify our requirements for admittance into the U.S.

I am sure my fellow panelists would agree that an 80 year old woman should not have to go through secondary screening at the airport before she gets on an airplane. Why? Because she is very unlikely to have a bomb or other weapon on her body. Is this not profiling? How many 80 year old female terrorists have you read about?

Exactly my point.

But these same panelists took issue with me for saying that America should deny entry and student visas for people from certain countries. Is it discriminatory? Yes. Is it appropriate and reasonable? Yes.

Does that mean every person from a country known to produce terrorists is a terrorist themselves? Of course not, but that is not the overriding issue in my decision to deny them entry into the U.S. I am sure there are many good people from countries that are known for producing terrorists; but I am not willing to take a chance, just for the sake of making Americans feel good, that this person is one of the good guys.

If you are the parent of a young boy, would you leave him alone with a Catholic priest? I wouldn't. I would venture to think that most Catholic priests are good people, but I am not willing to sacrifice my son's safety to prove a point.

The two brothers from Chechnya who committed the bombings in Boston should have never been allowed in the U.S. Is this an indictment of all people from Chechnya? No. It simply means that the U.S. is exercising its sovereignty to determine who is admitted into the U.S. This is a very reasonable and smart approach to our immigration policy. To do anything else is a reckless disregard for the future and safety of our country.

The Cartoonish College Republicans

Published: June 19, 2013

W hen I read the recently released report by The College Republican National Committee (CRNC), titled, "Grand Old Party for a Brand New Generation," I immediately thought of two cartoons: the Flintstones and the Jetsons.

The Flintstones was an animated, prime-time TV show that debuted in 1960. It was a cartoon about a working class family in the Stone Age.

The Jestons was a cartoon that debuted in 1962. The show was about a futuristic family who lived 100 years in the future (2062).

While the Flintstones lived in a world with machines powered by birds and dinosaurs, the Jetsons lived in a world of elaborate robotic contraptions, aliens, and holograms.

What was interesting about both cartoons was that there were no Blacks in either—so, we were not part of the past (Flintstones) and we were not part of the future (Jetsons).
As it was with the Flintstones and the Jetsons, so is it with the College Republicans, no Blacks anywhere to be found. How can you talk about the future of a major party organization and not say a word about the Black community?

According to their website, "the CRNC conducted six focus groups throughout the United States earlier this year with people from many different backgrounds who had previously voted for President Obama and did a poll of 800 registered voters."

The Politico Newspaper went on to say, "The report is based largely on two national surveys of 800 registered voters each, ages 18-29, and six focus groups of young people, including Hispanics, Asian-Americans, single women, economically struggling men and aspiring entrepreneurs in Ohio, Florida and California who had voted for President Barack Obama — he cleaned up with 60 percent of the youth vote — but were considered "winnable" for the GOP."

Did they talk to any Blacks in any of those focus groups? Were there any Blacks included in the polls? There is nothing in their report to indicate that they received input from any Blacks. I have yet to hear one mention of the Black community from the people involved in putting this report together.

The CRNC and Kristen Soltis Anderson of the Winston Group (who organized the focus groups and did the polling) have been all over the media high-fiving themselves, but never even mentioned the Black vote. The largest voting block for Obama was the Black community and no one talks to them? WOW!

Last week, I made several calls to Alex Smith, National Chair, CRNC, but never got a return call. But, in fairness to her, she was in the middle of final preparations for their national conference this past weekend in DC. I have no personal connection to her or the organization.

So, I went to the CRNC's website and noticed that they have no Blacks in leadership, not a Black in any photos on their site, and not one Black speaker during their conference this past weekend.

So, CRNC, let me make sure I understand. You criticize the direction of the national party, but yet you are doing the same thing you have accused the national party of doing—having no diversity, insensitive rhetoric, and no messaging that appeals to those outside the party or your group.
H-e-l-l-o. Can I introduce you to my friend pot calling the kettle black?

Can someone please tell me how the CRNC, in the 21st century, can continue to be a lily-white organization and expect to be relevant?

Did the CRNC really need to spend all this time, energy, and money to state the obvious—that they have the same problem as the Republican National Committee (RNC)?

Priebus, chair of the RNC, seems to be the only one in party leadership that understands what needs to be done and he has actually put his money where his mouth is. He has hired minority staffers, given them budgetary and hiring authority; he is open to new thoughts and ideas; and he is committed to changing the face of the RNC.

The House, Senate, and CRNC leadership should be following the same blueprint that Priebus is using. I am stunned that the CRNC has no Blacks in any photos on their website and none in leadership (they have one Latino).

But, what is more insulting to me, as a Black Republican, is that the CRNC is probably totally oblivious to the fact that they have no Blacks involved in the group; that they have no Blacks speaking during their conference; or that they said nothing about the Black vote in their report.

It is very easy to help a person with a problem when they acknowledge they have a problem; but what do you do when the person is not aware that they have a problem?

So, to the CRNC, we, in the Black community, have already played the role of the Flintstones in the past of your organization; and in your just released report, we are playing the role of the Jetsons, not in your future.

Is this really the role you want the Black community to continue to play in your organization—no past and no future?

Supreme Court Made Right Call on Voting and Affirmative Action

Published: July 2, 2013

L ast week liberal Blacks and whites went crazy after the Supreme Court issued its ruling on Affirmative Action and the Voting Rights cases.

Well, I happen to agree with the court in both decisions. Now, before you Black liberals start calling me a "sell-out, Uncle Tom, or Republican," turn off your emotions and listen to reason.

In the Black community, the mere mention of revisiting any Civil Rights program automatically elicits cries of "Jim Crow," "racism," or "turning back the clock."

Despite protestations to the contrary, in a 7-1 decision, the Supreme Court actually upheld the use of Affirmative Action. They simply stated that institutions must prove that they have exhausted all other remedies before they resort to using race in their admission decisions. In light of the progress we have made in this country on the issue of race, I find the court's decision very reasonable.

What I did find troubling about this case brought by a white high school student, Abigail Fisher; was her assertion of "white privilege." She is from Sugar Land, TX (one of the wealthiest communities in TX). She sued the University of Texas at Austin after she was denied admission to the school in 2008. According to her, "it was because she was white and that she was being treated differently than some less-qualified minority students who were accepted."

Of course she has no way of knowing that since the admissions process is confidential. But, she just assumes that because she is white and from Sugar Land; there is no way that a minority could be more qualified than she for admission to the school. In written submissions to the Court, the school stated that even without the issue of affirmative action, Fisher did not meet the school's standards for admission. She is "white privilege" personified.

The Civil Rights community totally lost their minds over the Voting Rights case, though the Court upheld the status quo. The Court simply said that Congress needed to redo the formula that determines which states should remain under the supervision of the Department of Justice.

Let me explain it this way. In the 60's & 70's, polyester suits were in vogue. What the Court said was, it's the 21st century so we think you might need to change the fabric used in your suits. You can still have whatever suit you want, you simply need to update the material you are using to one that is more appropriate to the times. Again, I find this very reasonable.

So, to Civil Rights icons like John Lewis and Julian Bond— c-h-i-l-l-o-u-t! If you listen to them and the liberal media, you would have thought the Supreme Court put Blacks back in chains.

We must approach these decisions strategically, not emotionally. In a weird kind of way, I am very optimistic that Republicans will step up and play a constructive role in facilitating a thoughtful discussion of these two important court decisions.

The key players on these two issues will be, House Majority Whip White Eric Cantor and Congressman Jim

Sensenbrenner. Cantor represents the 10th district of Virginia in the U.S. House of Representatives. He instinctively gets and understands the issue of race better than most Republicans. He has quite an interesting story to tell in this regard and I hope one day soon he will allow me to share his story with the public.

Sensenbrenner represents Wisconsin's 5th congressional district and is former Chairman of the House's Judiciary Committee. He has been a stalwart on issues revolving around Civil Rights, specifically the reauthorization of the Voting Rights Act in 2006.

If Speaker of the House, John Boehner, taps Cantor and Sensenbrenner into playing key roles in helping the Republican Party understand some of these issues involving race, I am fairly confident that they will lead the party down a constructive path that will show the Black community that Republicans understand these two issues that are of great interest to the Black community. There is a lot of work to be done in this regard in the U.S. Senate; but Cantor and Sensenbrenner's unique understanding on these issues can be a great asset if the party's leaders take advantage of it.

CHAPTER 5

❧ AFRICA ❧

INTRODUCTION BY:

General William E. "Kip" Ward, U.S. Army (Ret.), Inaugural Commander, United States Africa Command.

After meeting Raynard a few years ago at an Africa Policy Forum where we both were speakers, I have enjoyed knowing him on a personal basis. Being exposed to his wide circle of friends and contacts has been a privilege.

Raynard has devoted several of his columns over the years to outlining and conveying an understanding of the set of activities that characterize the interactions, or lack thereof, between the continent of Africa (and their various leaders) with the political and business leadership of the United States.

This section highlights a portion of those activities leaving you, the reader, with a sense of his understanding of the pitfalls, strengths, weaknesses, and stereotypes of the complex web of U.S. – African dynamics. Whether you find yourself agreeing with Raynard's assertions and conclusions or otherwise, you will find a consistent theme—better and more engagement.

The relationships that are described and their significance will strike the reader as an essential factor in this complex dynamic. Each column written addressed the nature of the relationship that exists between African leaders and the American public. These articles highlighted gaps in those relationships as well as the misunderstandings that were evident between Africans and the American public, especially Black Americans, due to gaps, lack of attention, lack of focus, and sporadic commitment to relationship building. Without effective relationship building, the prospects for understanding and further advances between our cultures are bleak.

Raynard's description of African initiatives that are not adequately promoted and publicized in the United States prevent us from taking advantage of them in dismissing or neutralizing historically negative and uninformed images of Africa. He criticizes African leaders for failing to embrace the Black American community in conveying the positive story of Africa and the opportunities (business and cultural) on the continent. Beneath this, he conveys a notion that Africans somehow have less than a favorable perception of Black Americans and offers a reason for this as possibly fueled by those who stand to gain from presenting this unfavorable characterization. Mr. Jackson highlights the tendency of U.S. political elites to critique African leaders on their social justice stances while failing to do the same for other non-African nations.

Raynard's writings are interesting and provocative. And even in not agreeing with all his assertions, the conclusions provide much for reflection.

The African and the Brother Man

Published: August 6, 2009

I received a call from a good friend of mine earlier this week. He's a Black gentleman who worked very high in the Clinton administration. He's one of the top political operatives in the country.

He called me because he wanted to get together and talk. He was extremely frustrated with his dealings with African leaders. He asked me why African governments seems to always hire white lobbying firms to represent them in the U.S., but then ask Black's to join them in the struggle to make Africa more stable?

Having done a lot of work in African countries for various presidents, I have often wondered the same thing. So, I began calling other friends with various levels of knowledge and familiarity with Africa. My friend's experience was very common among most of those I talked with.

Part of the problem is that African's think the "white man's" ice is colder than the "Black man's ice." Last time I checked my chemistry book, water freezes at 32 degrees, regardless of who puts the water into the freezer.

One thing I have learned and noticed during my many trips to Africa is a lot of these attitudes are taught to Africans. They are taught that Black Americans are not serious people, they are criminals, and they should not be trusted. Most African's only image of Blacks come from BET or the Hip-Hop community.

Two weeks ago I had a heated conversation with a friend of mine from Ethiopia. She has been in the U.S. for about 10 years. I asked her has she ever dated a Black American. She emphatically said, "NO, and I never will!" It was not only what she said, but the disdain in her tone of voice. It was though the very thought of dating a Black American was repulsive to her. When asked why, she said because they are not Ethiopian (she doesn't date outside her culture). I told her she sounds just like some of the good ole boys from the south when it comes to Blacks dating white women and her comment was simply idiotic. Is discrimination based on culture equivalent to discrimination based on race? I will be dedicating one of my radio shows to this issue very soon.

I cannot count the number of times I have had to challenge my treatment by Africans in my own country! I am amazed how many Africans are surprised that I can speak with knowledge about many countries on the continent. When they hear me discuss local issues that one can only know if they have been to a given country, their whole attitude changes.

What does it say about how Africans view Blacks when a very connected political operative can't get a contract to represent an African country? You would have thought that Obama's election would have shifted that dynamic somewhat, but it hasn't. But, as soon as African's get in trouble, they run to the Congressional Black Caucus for relief. The CBC should tell them in no uncertain terms, "when you hire some Blacks to work with you, then come see me." I have seen white elected officials do this on many occasions when it comes to their own.

I have donated thousands of dollars' worth of professional services to African causes and charities only to have them contract with others once they get money. I now refuse to deal with any African cause or issue unless there is a budget for professional services.

So, when my friend expressed his frustration with me, I could definitely relate to his situation. Until Africans change their attitude towards Blacks in America, there will always be a rift between the two groups.

This attitude is the underlying reason that the continent has not progressed more than it has. Africa has everything it needs to sustain the continent and be truly independent. But, they can't continue to beg others to do for them what they are not willing to do for themselves. They want Black entrepreneurs to invest in their country, but refuse to hire Blacks who can assist them in making this happen. One of the largest IT firms in the world is owned by a Black, one of the larger restaurant owners in the country is owned by a Black, some of the best medical professionals in this country are Black, and some of the best architects and engineers in this country are Black. So, then why does Africa refuse to recognize this with their dollars? How many African presidents have ever given a speech at a Black college, visited a Black business owner's company, or visited a Black media company? The answer is very few.

So, to my Africans both here and on the continent, don't call me "Brother" and then give all the opportunity to others. Don't call me "Brother" only when you need help. Africa is where it all started and where our ancestors departed. So, when you come to the U.S., when will you recognize your own family? BROTHER!

The AfrICAN and the AmerICAN

Published: August 27, 2009

Earlier this month I wrote a column entitled, **"The African and the Brother Man.** I had no idea my piece would spark such a vibrant conversation among Blacks, Africans, Caribbeans, and others. Some agreed with what I wrote and others did not. Some agreed with me, but had issues with my verbiage. But, as legendary composer Quincy Jones told rapper Ice-T, "Ice, keep doin what you're doin, man don't give a damn if the squares don't understand. You let em tell you what to say and what to write, your whole career'll be over by tomorrow night."

Therefore, based on the volume of emails received and the level of interest in me establishing a platform for dialogue, I decided to devote my whole show this Saturday to this issue. I will have live guests from Africa, America, and the Caribbean to begin the conversation. Then we will open the phone lines to callers from around the world. We will also have a live chat room for people to submit questions and comments.

The show will focus on the "Ican" in African and American. We want this to be the beginning of a conversation that will lead to a reduction in the barriers existing between these communities. Issues and questions that I want to deal with are: why did my Ethiopian friend say to me that she would **NEVER** date a Black American?

Why do African and Caribbean governments rarely give lobbying contracts to Black Americans? Why are African and Caribbean tourism TV commercials always focused on the white community (Bahamas, Jamaica, Trinidad, South Africa, Ghana)? Why do most Blacks think of jungles or Tarzan when asked about Africa? Why do African or Caribbean ambassadors and embassies have NO presence in the Black community, locally or nationally?

By the end of the show, I hope we have addressed these concerns and have found ways that we can move forward with closing the gap that exists between these communities.

Hopefully, we can get some of these ambassadors to host a series of after work networking receptions for people to mix and mingle with each other.

I would love to create a speaker's series where I can provide a platform for their visiting president to address various audiences in the U.S.

I have offered to have several African and Caribbean presidents on my radio show, but none have taken advantage of my offer to speak directly to the American people. Typically, you only see or hear them in the American media when something negative has happened in their countries. Let us be proactive and talk about the good that is going on in their respective countries.

These are some of my solutions to the above identified problems. I know I can deliver on my end, but are the various countries willing to take advantage of my offer? When it comes to offering solutions, **I CAN!**

The U.S.A.--It's About Time

Published: September 24, 2009

I s it finally time for a United States of Africa (U.S.A.) to emerge? Without question, I think the time is right. But, it's about time also. I was once in Africa meeting with the president of a country and he basically said his "house was on fire." So, I said to this president that I had the water that could extinguish the fire. His response? "I will let you know when I want the water."

This has been a common experience with me in my dealings on the continent. Africans have their own concept of time and in most cases it is not congruous with the major powers of the world.

Last week I attended a speech by H.E. Cheikh Tidiane Gadio, Senior Minister & Minister of Foreign Affairs from the Republic of Senegal. The purpose of his speech was to discuss the concept of a United States of Africa. He was a great speaker, with a thorough knowledge of the subject matter. Whether you were an academic or layman, the minister displayed the communication skills necessary to make the concept understandable to everyone. I was most impressed with the minister.

A united Africa makes all the sense in the world. After all, Europe has done it, South American is doing, and of course the United States is the model for how to do it. According to the minister, they have 20 countries that are ready to move forward, with the other 33 hesitating for one reason or another.

Logistical, political, and economic hurdles aside, I see a major strategic flaw in the minister's approach. Africa has yet to lay out the intellectual arguments for the movement in the U.S. and Europe. Though these two groups can't vote on the proposal, I think it is in Africa's interest to educate the general public as to the relevance of this movement.

For example, when I go to see my orthodontist, Dr. Larry Kawa (www.braces1.com), I know exactly what is going to happen. The staffer assigned to me, Linda, is the best. Before she starts, she tells me what the purpose of this particular visit is, what she is going to do, why she is going to do it, and the expected result from that day's visit. If there are any changes to the treatment for that visit, she will explain why the change occurred and why it is necessary.

My point is, an educated patient is the best patient. So it is relative to the U.S.A., an educated world is the best world.

Discussion of a united Africa is no new thing. Marcus Garvey is credited with being the father of a united Africa as early as 1924. He was way ahead of his time and the issue is still being debated within the continent.

So, I think the minister, specifically and Africa in general, must do a better job in educating the U.S. as to why Africa matters to us. Why should a proposed United State of Africa matter to the diaspora within the U.S.?

The time for Africa to unite is now, but the time to educate strategic allies is also now. I find most African embassies have very little presence within the U.S. This is not all African embassies, but a lot of them do fit into this category. They should be more engaged in the local communities, as well as the various media outlets. Most of the images you see regarding Africa are about war, famine, and despair. I put most of the blame on African nations for not countering these images conjured up by the media.

Africa has a lot of positive stories to tell, but they must not wait or depend on someone else to tell their story. They must persist in their efforts to force American media do show the positive side of Africa. Most Americans have little appreciation as to how close Africa is to the U.S.

For example, most people don't realize that from the east coast, you can get to Dakar, Senegal in about the same time it's takes to get to Los Angeles or San Francisco! So, if I have a 4 day weekend, I would much rather go to Senegal than I would Los Angeles or San Francisco.

Most people don't know that most of the world's diamonds come from Africa, as does cocoa. Africa has the world's largest population of people under 18. This group will have tremendous purchasing power in the years to come.

China, Europe, and the U.S. are getting older. Africa is getting younger. Every businessman knows what this means—Africa is the next "MTV" generation (for better and for worse). So, if Africa could unite and harness this potential and all the natural assets it possesses, they can and will be a power to reckon with.

While they are working on resolving the many logistical impediments to unification, on a parallel track, they must launch a strategic educational campaign simultaneously.

To do otherwise is like baking a cake without preheating the oven. You will get a cake, but all the ingredients will not have blended together as they should have.

So, educating Europe, Asia, and the U.S. is the preheating process. When I say educate, I am speaking of going directly to the people, not the "powers that be." So, to the proposed United States of Africa, it's about time!

A Heavenly Thought

Published: September 16, 2010

E verybody wants to go to heaven, but no one wants to die. I have been told that the only way to go to heaven without dying is by visiting the beautiful island of the Seychelles (pronounced— say-chells).

It is an island country consisting of 115 smaller (mostly uninhabited) islands. It is located off the east coast of Africa (northeast of Madagascar) in the middle of the Indian Ocean. It has a small population, just over 87,000 people; but is big on hospitality.

President James Michel has made a serious investment in his country's most valued asset—it's people. They speak Creole, French and English. With tourism being their largest source of revenue, he has impressed upon his people the importance of being great hosts to all visitors.

President Michel has also put in place a solid infrastructure to ensure the long term economic and political viability of his country for years to come.

Now that President Michel has gotten his "internal" house in order, he is looking outward. The Seychelles is launching a series of Investment Forums in different countries. The first one will be next Tuesday in New York City in the U.S. I was asked by a friend, Mr. Peter Sinon, to help organize this event. The Honorable Peter Sinon is the Minister of Investments & Natural Resources. He last served his country as Executive Director of the African Development Bank.

Over the past year, I have become more aware of the possibilities of the Seychelles expanding its presence as a destination spot for American tourists. With them having a very stable government and economy, they are also a fertile country for possible investments.

America presents a great, untapped market for the Seychelles in terms of additional tourists, but also as new sources of investment.

Most Americans have never heard of the Seychelles and most have never visited. I strongly encourage the country to develop an awareness campaign to educate Americans to the opportunities present within the Seychelles.

Americans have millions of high net worth individuals, celebrities, athletes, and businessmen who can well afford to take their vacations (holidays) in this beautiful country. But, thus far, there has been no effort by the Seychelles to reach out to this population of Americans.

I think their upcoming Investment Forum is a great first step. It will be in Tribeca, in lower Manhattan, New York. They have a high powered delegation coming to the U.S. It is being led by their Vice President, Mr. Danny Faure, the President of the African Development Bank, Mr. Donald Kaberuka, and Mr. Peter Sinon, to name a few.

Because of air travel, the world is constantly shrinking and we are becoming a more global society. Americans, because of our wealth, have a plethora of choices when it comes to discretionary dollars for vacations (holidays).

It is incumbent upon the Seychelles to increase its visibility to targeted demographic groups within the U.S. This can best be accomplished with a well thought out marketing campaign that touts the virtues of making the Seychelles a **must see** destination!

Just imagine having the best of both worlds: going to heaven without dying. Can you say Seychelles? I can!

Banking on Africa

Published: September 30, 2009

The only images most Americans see on U.S. media about Africa is that of famine, war, or other tragedies. But, with a little effort, another view of Africa begins to emerge.

Last week I had the honor of spending a few days with the Honorable Peter Sinon, Executive Director of the African Development Bank.

The goal of the African Development Bank (AfDB) Group is to create sustainable economic development and social progress in its regional member countries (RMCs), thereby helping to reduce poverty. This is achieved by mobilizing and allocating resources for investment in RMCs & providing policy advice and technical assistance to support development efforts.

The bank might help in the financing of road construction, building of dams, or the financing of mining projects. It might also help to fund the operational budget of a particular country. The bank might also partner with the World Bank to promote trade and investment liberalization and the privatization of state-owned companies, thereby creating local jobs.

According to the bank's website, "The major rating agencies Moody's, Standard & Poor's, Fitch and the Japanese Credit Rating Agency have assigned a triple-A rating on AfDB long term senior debt and double A-plus on its subordinated debt. The outlook on all the ratings are stable and reflect the Bank's strong membership support, healthy capital adequacy, preferred creditor status and strong financial condition." How many stories about this have you seen on the U.S. news? I understand that the AfDB is still considered a small player on the continent in the area of finance (they provide about 6% of total development assistance on the continent, about U.S. $ 3 billion annually). But, their goal is not to compete with the World Bank (one of the dominant players on the continent).

Spending time with Mr. Sinon, I am not only more aware of the role and mission of the bank, but also very optimistic about it's (and the continent's) future. Mr. Sinon is more than just another highly trained economist. He clearly understands that economic theories must be practical and able to provide measurable change in the lives of people.

Mr. Sinon also sang the praises of the bank's president, Mr. Donald Kaberuka, the former Finance Minister of Rwanda. He was elected president in 2005 and is up for reelection next year (he is expected to win another 5 year term). He has brought much needed vision and focus to the bank and under his leadership, the bank is playing a much larger role on the continent.

Under Mr. Kaberuka's leadership, the bank expects its investments in 2009 to double with commitments amounting to around US $ 11 billion from US $ 5.8 billion last year.

How many reading this column knew that Mr. Kaberuka was in the U.S. last week? Last Monday he rang the closing bell on Wall Street. Afterword he gave the keynote address at the Africa Investor Index Series Summit and Awards at the exchange. He also attended the 2009 Annual Meeting of the Clinton Global Initiative; spoke at the G20 Summit in Pittsburgh, and participated in a meeting with the Congressional Black Caucus Foundation.

I think Mr. Kaberuka and the bank should plan a program in the U.S. that would allow him to educate Americans about the bank and its role in the development of Africa. This program should have a media component—have interviews with majority & ethnic newspapers, TV programs, and radio programs. I would also include several speeches at universities and professional financial organizations (National Associating of Black Money Managers, etc.).

Mr. Keberuka has a great story to tell. Under his leadership, that bank is investing larger amounts on the continent, becoming more influential, becoming more focused, and being recognized as a well-run organization.

Mr. Keberuka can't expect the images coming out of Africa to change on it's on. He must become more aggressive about championing the successes of his bank. That will require him to become more media savvy.

With his leadership and that of Mr. Peter Sinon, I think their organization is something that the continent of African can bank on.

AfriCan

Published: September 30, 2010

D uring the past two weeks I have been asked to be involved in two projects relating to Africa. While dealing with Africa can sometimes be very frustrating, after the past two weeks, I am very high on the future of Africa.

Last month I was asked to help put together the first ever Seychelles Investment Forum in New York. The event was held last week and was a great success. The Seychelles is off the east coast of Africa, surrounded by the Indian Ocean (www.seychellesembassy.com).

After the Seychelles event, I then had the opportunity to participate on a panel during the African Policy Forum, hosted by the Leon H. Sullivan Foundation in Atlanta, GA.

I have been flying back and forth to the continent for many years, but this immersion in all things Africa has restored my optimism in the future of the continent.

The Seychelles event was an opportunity for American businessmen and media professionals to become acquainted with investment possibilities and to learn more about this quiet, tropical paradise.

The delegation was led by the vice president of the Seychelles, the Honorable Danny Faure. He is simultaneously serving as the minister of finance. Relatively young, he has lots of experience within government. He is extremely personable and has the charm of Bill Clinton. I see him being a "fix-it" man throughout the continent in the future. Remember his name. You will hear it many times in the future.

Other members of the delegation included ministers Peter Sinon (Investments, Natural Resources and Industry), Jean-Paul Adam (Foreign Affairs), and their permanent representative to the United Nations & ambassador to the U.S., the honorable Ronny Jumeau.

Mr. Sinon is a former executive director for the African Development Bank. He is a great strategic thinker and has an enviable rolodex of friends that spans the globe. I hope his president, James Michel, takes full advantage of Mr. Sinon's great mind and rolodex. I am a political animal at heart, thus had a great time talking global politics with Mr. Adam. He reminds me greatly of our former secretary of state, James A. Baker. He has worked within various levels of the government and is a close personal advisor to the president. Mr. Jumeau is the well-seasoned statesman that is very comfortable with change and has the uncanny ability to bridge the gap between the old and the young. He definitely has the skill set to be a great diplomat.

Gregory Simpkins (vice president of the Leon H. Sullivan Foundation and one of the foremost experts on Africa in the entire U.S.) asked me to participate on a panel called "The Media's Africa May Not Be Your Africa: Exploring Fact and Fiction." This was part of the Sullivan Foundation's Africa Policy Forum in Atlanta, GA.

The goal of the foundation is to "bring the corporate and governmental communities together for the economic benefit of all, and invite businesses and individuals to create partnerships with Africa with our ultimate goal being a peaceful, prosperous, and powerful Africa."

The foundation is led by Ms. Hope Sullivan Masters (daughter of the great Leon Sullivan). She has taken the organization from a dream to reality. She put together one of the most substantive programs on Africa I have ever been a part of.

As I indicated on the panel, African leaders should not expect the American media to accurately portray the totality of all the continent has to offer. Typically the media only show stories that deal with famine, war, or poverty. They never show the great education system of Botswana, the middle class wealth of Nigeria, or the modernity of Ethiopia.

But, I also faulted African heads of state for not building relations with Black media in the U.S. How many African leaders have ever been interviewed by Black newspaper owners, magazines, or blogs?

To my amazement, even former U.N. ambassador Andy Young and former Nigerian president, Olusegun Obasanjo agreed with my assessment.

President Obasanjo, now an elder statesman, is a travelling trouble shooter throughout the continent. He is called on by world bodies to mediate various conflicts on behalf of the U.N., the African Union, etc.

I had the opportunity to spend some private time with him in his suite this past weekend. He is a remarkable, walking history of Africa. I hope my good friend Isaiah Washington (former star of Grey's Anatomy) will one day do a film on the life of president Obasanjo.

I have known Isaiah a few years now and can visibly see the transformation that he has undergone since he began his travels back and forth to the continent. He served as honorary chairman of the African Policy Forum. You can see and feel the spirit of our ancestors speaking through him when he talks about Africa. One of my favorite scriptures from the Bible came to mind when I was listening to him. Ironically enough, it is Isaiah 61:1-2: *"The Spirit of the Lord God is upon me; because the Lord hath anointed me to preach good tidings unto the meek; he hath sent me to bind up the brokenhearted, to proclaim liberty to the captives, and the opening of the prison to them that are bound; to proclaim the acceptable year of the Lord, and the day of vengeance of our Got; to comfort all that mourn."*

Expect Isaiah to be one of the leading voices on Africa during the next generation.

With young leaders being groomed for the future in the Seychelles; with elder statesmen like President Obasanjo imparting his wisdom to the next generation; and voices like Isaiah Washington conjuring up spirits from our ancestors, you should understand why it is up to all of us to put the can in AfriCan!

Macy's Proves AfriCan

Published: October 7, 2010

C an you imagine Michael Jordan hitting the game winning shot and then asking the media not to say anything? Or Barack Obama winning the presidential election and refusing to talk about his victory? Or You discovering the cure for cancer, but not wanting anyone to know?

Well, that's in essence what Macy's Department Stores have done. Macy's is the top department store chain in the U.S., with more than 800 stores in 45 states and annual sales of more than $26 billion.

Two weeks ago I was a speaker at the Leon H. Sullivan Foundation's Africa Policy Forum in Atlanta, Georgia. Macy's was one of the sponsors and I had the chance to meet and talk with their representative, Ms. Iasha Rivers. She is their director of external affairs & corporate communications.

I asked Ms. Rivers why Macy's is a sponsor of the Sullivan Foundation and she began to give me a very passionate response. She gave me the history of Macy's "Rwanda Path to Peace" basket project. The project was begun in July 2005.

According to Macy's, "The Rwanda Path to Peace project was established to create a viable, sustainable export business that provides economic stability and promotes an environment of peace that will positively influence Rwanda's future for its 8 million citizens. Its basic concept is that women helping each other can change the way Rwanda rebuilds its society, empowering women and sustaining economic development beyond traditional development assistance. The women receive one-third of the retail price of the baskets -- an unprecedented amount of income for individual rural households. The project has the potential to generate millions of dollars for the country, positively affecting the millions of Rwandans who normally live on less than $1 a day."

Baskets woven by the women are exported to the US and sold exclusively at Macy's Department Store. They are the number one export out of Rwanda under the African Growth and Opportunity Act (AGOA).

Macy's was adamant that, "this may have been charitable, but it was not charity." They continued, "baskets, woven from sisal and sweet grass, are inspected to verify they meet quality requirements and then paid for in cash on the spot."

With the phenomenal success of the Rwanda Path to Peace basket project, Macy's created Shop for a better World in 2008. This is a collection of artisans from Africa, Indonesia, and Cambodia who make one-of-a-kind crafts (all hand-made).

Shop for a Better World is a partnership between Macy's and Fair Winds Trading, which was founded by Willa Shalit, a social activist and entrepreneur.

Shop for a Better World is a vertically integrated operation; all steps of production take place in the origin country using only raw materials sourced from the region. The program employs a large population of women who live in the rural countryside, allowing them to maintain their current residence and avoid the often costly and disruptive process of relocating to cities in search of work.

Listening to Ms. Rivers share this story with me, I couldn't hide my astonishment that such a storied company as Macy's had undertaken such a project and I had no knowledge of it. I am a frequent traveler to Africa and consider myself one who follows the goings on in Africa. But, if people like me are unaware of what Macy's is doing, how much more the general public?

Macy's and their CEO, Terry Lundgren should be lauded and commended for finding a business approach to helping Africa. But, I am somewhat confused as to why Macy's hasn't built an advertising campaign around this partnership with the women of Rwanda. This is an advertising gold mine!

Having spent years of my life in "corporate America" before starting my own firm, I have a pretty good idea as to why Macy's executives are hesitant to talk about their partnership with Rwanda. The short answer is that this story has a "racial" angle to it. Macy's senior executives are probably all white and they are terrified at the prospects of being viewed as "using" this story to toot their own horn for profit.

Well, Macy's made it perfectly clear that this was a "business" arrangement, not charity. What retail operation would not want to publicize a remarkable success story that is actually making a difference in the lives of people who have had a tragic past? Macy's has found a profitable way of exporting the American dream to the continent of Africa.

They should be asked to testify before Congress about how this partnership came about. I think Macy's should have Ms. Rivers bring some of the women from Rwanda to the U.S. for a series of town hall meetings about how this arrangement with Macy's has impacted their lives and their country. If Macy's won't tell the story, then I will. I will use all of my media outlets to tout this wonderful story that Macy's has created.

So, to all of my readers world-wide, I want you to express your support for what Macy's is doing directly to their CEO, Mr. Terry Lundgren. You can reach him at his corporate offices in Cincinnati, Ohio at: 513-579-7000. I couldn't find a general email address for Macy's, but if you email me your thoughts, I will forward them directly to Ms. Rivers.

I don't normally shop at Macy's, but as a result of what they are doing on the continent, that will change effective this weekend. I will not only buy the baskets from Rwanda, but I will also do more of my regular retail shopping there. If Macy's can support the continent, then I can support Macy's and I encourage all of my readers to do the same. Macy's has proven that AfriCAN!

Africa Needs More Good Luck

Published: January 6, 2011

Current Nigerian President, Goodluck Jonathan is considered a rising star among many in the international community. Good luck seems to be the hallmark of his life.

He ascended to the presidency last year with the untimely death of his predecessor, Umaru Yar'Adua. Mr. Jonathan, a zoologist by training, is not your typical Nigerian politician.

Upon completing his education, he worked as an education inspector, professor, and environmental protection officer. He has only been involved in politics since 1998. He served as Deputy Governor of Bayelsa State in 1998 before becoming governor later that year. The incumbent governor was impeached on charges of money laundering.

In 2006, Jonathan was chosen by Yar'Adua as his vice presidential running mate and they won election in 2007. In 2010, during his role as acting president of Nigeria (while Yar'Adua was medically incapacitated), Jonathan was elected chairman of the Economic Community of West African States (ECOWAS). ECOWAS is a regional group of 15 West African countries founded in 1975. Its mission is to promote economic integration across the region, as well as to serve as a peacekeeping force in the region.

Since becoming president, Jonathan is seen as being totally committed to eradicating the culture of corruption that has plagued Nigeria for most of its existence. He is well thought of by the international community and his own people seem to be very optimistic about his leadership.

Jonathan is facing reelection in April. As of this writing, he is expected to win reelection, but in politics, fortunes change very quickly.

This is why I am quite surprised that Jonathan has not taken advantage of the platform he has as chairman of ECOWAS. They have been the lead mediator in the current post election controversy in Cote D'Ivoire (a West African country with Liberia to the west and Ghana to the east). The current president of Cote D'Ivoire, Laurent

Gbagbo refuses to abdicate his office even though every neutral observer has concluded that he lost the election.

Jonathan has been given the opportunity to demonstrate his leadership on the world's stage, but he seems a bit shy about injecting himself; instead he is delegating the heavy lifting to other members of ECOWAS.

Politically, this is a huge mistake. If he is seen as major instrument for peace in a country like Cote D'Ivoire, he can then make the argument that he has the same skills to bring peace to his own country of Nigeria.

This is a goldmine for a political consultant—to have a client who can use a foreign crisis to bolster his own standing back home this close to an election. There is no downside to Jonathan for his personal engagement. He would be acting as the leader of ECOWAS, not as president of Nigeria.

Jonathan has made very few public comments during this crisis, but rather, allowing others to speak on behalf of ECOWAS. I find this is not uncommon for African leaders. They don't seem to fully grasp the necessity of engaging the global media in their efforts to affect public opinion.

Africans constantly complain about how they are portrayed in the world, especially in the U.S. and Europe, but they never pursue a media strategy to change this.

Jonathan has a bright future, not only in Nigeria, but also on the world stage. He is a very likable person with a great deal of charm. But, he is going to have to display more political and media savvy. If he learns to appreciate the role of the media in the pursuit of his agenda, he can not only bring good luck to himself, but more Goodluck to Africa.

Is Visiting Africa A Stretch?

Published: January 13, 2011

O liver Wendell Holmes, Sr. (father of the former Chief Justice of the U.S. Supreme Court with the same name) once stated, "A mind that is stretched to a new idea never returns to its original dimensions."

I think the sooner African leaders come to understand this, the better off the continent will be. Every time I meet with African leaders, they always complain about how Africa is portrayed in the U.S. media. But yet, they never seem to understand the need to have a media strategy in place to be proactive in the promotion of how they want Africa to be portrayed.

Tourism provides the best example of this. African leaders want more investment from U.S. companies and individuals, but before that can happen, there must be an educational campaign. Tourism is the best way to educate Americans about Africa. Simply put, there is no replacement for actually going to the continent and living the experience. To put it another way, Africa must **BRAND** the continent in a positive manner.

Before you can convince more Americans about the virtues of investing in Africa, Americans must be stripped of the images they have of Africa—one of poverty, instability, famine, war, etc. While each of these pathologies is present in Africa, so is the reverse. You have a country like Botswana, where all the proceeds from their diamond mines are used to give their citizens free education all the way through university. Not even America does this for its citizens. You have Ghana as one of the most stable economies on the continent. You have South Africa with its own stock market that is booming.

You have a lot of success throughout the continent, but Africa must not wait for anyone to tell their story. They must tell their own story!

How many Americans understand that from the east coast of the U.S. you can be in Dakar, Senegal in about the same time it would take to get to Los Angeles or San Francisco?

Why has Senegal, Delta Airlines, or the Le Meridian Hotel (a fiver star hotel in Senegal) not educated Americans to this fact?

How many Americans know that Delta Airlines flies nonstop from Atlanta to Senegal, Accra, Ghana, and Lagos, Nigeria?

How many Americans know that the most profitable route, world-wide, of Delta Airlines is Atlanta to Lagos?

I consider tourism a national security issue for Africa. The best way to fight terrorism is by exposure. The more tourists that visit Africa, the more difficult it is to paint the west as anti-African or anti-Muslim. When Africans get the chance to interact and engage with American tourists, the more difficult it will be to make people hate—because they have had the opportunity to meet a foreigner at the hotel, at the market, at the shop!

The faster Africa understands the value of educating Americans about the continent and gives us reason to visit their countries, the sooner Americans will drop the stereotypes we have about Africa. Americans will realize there is no Tarzan or Jane in Africa, that Africans do wear clothes, or that Africa does have hotels with air conditioning.

An increase in tourism to Africa, will lead to a better understanding of Africa by Americans. Once Americans see the potential and possibilities of Africa, then, and only then, will an increase in investment happen.

So, to my African friends, the next time you complain about how the continent is portrayed in the U.S. media; ask yourself, what has your country done to educate America about your country? Ask yourself, why your president never meets with Black and other minority journalists when they are in the U.S.? Ask yourself why your minister of tourism never meets with Black tour operators and other minority travel professionals in the U.S.?

Stretching is very uncomfortable. But, by stretching before you work out at the gym, you minimize the possibility of injuring yourself during your workout. No one likes stretching, but everyone likes the result of stretching—an in shape, healthy body.

So, how much more with Africa? If Africa is willing to stretch itself into a more constructive engagement with Americans, then Americans will never return to its original stereotypes about Africa. Sometimes it might be a little uncomfortable for both sides. But, the result will be more business investment in Africa, more trade, and less conflict.

If African leaders follow my prescription, Africa will benefit immensely and we will realize that the distance between the continent and the U.S. is very small.

So, in my view, visiting Africa is not a stretch.

Can Africa Make The Cut

Published: April 21, 2011

Whenever the U.S. government enters into a state of fiscal austerity, politicians always look for budget cuts from programs they deem to be less important or have little or no constituency. Foreign policy budgets, especially those directed towards Africa seem to always show up near the top of that list.

The left will blame it on the "mean" Republicans who don't care about Africa. The truth is that Africa seems to benefit more from Republican control of Congress/White House than from Democratic control. Isn't it amazing that former President George W. Bush did more for Africa than any president in the history of the U.S.? But, yet, he gets little or no credit for his policies towards Africa.

It was the Bush administration that first labeled what was going on in the Sudan as genocide (made by then Secretary of State, Colin Powell before the Senate Foreign Relations Committee). Bush played a critical role in helping to end the civil war in the Sudan.

Under the Bush administration, development aid to Africa quadrupled from $ 1.3 billion in 2001 to more than $ 5 billion in 2008. The Millennium Challenge Corporation (MCC) was created by Bush. Africa has received in excess of $ 3.5 billion from the fund so far. The MCC was established to reward poor countries that encouraged economic growth, good governance, and social services for its citizens.

The Africa Growth and Opportunity Act (AGOA) was created in 2000 and expanded under Bush in 2004. The bill provides trade benefits with the U.S. for 40 African countries that have implemented reforms in their countries to encourage economic growth.

The President's Emergency Plan for AIDS Relief (PEPFAR) was created by Bush and had $ 15 billion appropriated over five years (2003-2008). I find it amazing that the program has been cut by the Obama administration (though Obama pledged to increase it by $ 1 billion annually during his presidential campaign).

Along with PEPFAR, Bush established the U.S. Leadership Against HIV/AIDS, Tuberculosis, and Malaria Act of 2003 (or the Global AIDS Act) established the State Department Office of the Global AIDS Coordinator to oversee all international AIDS funding and programming

Bush's policies are credited with saving the lives of millions of Africans. The political right would argue that America just can't afford to continue some of these programs. They don't question the merits of the programs, just the financial ability of the U.S. to continue to fund them.

I put the blame for this type of myopic thinking on two groups. The first is U.S. supporters of these programs (this includes, politicians, faith based groups, American citizens, etc.). America must do a better job in explaining why and how these programs impact the U.S. If we don't spend the money on the front end (for prevention), we will spend the money on the back end (for treatment, humanitarian intervention, nation building, etc.).

I would put most of the responsibility on the second group—African heads of state and their designated U.S. ambassadors! African leaders and their ambassadors show very little understanding of how to get things done through our political process here in Washington, DC. Most African ambassadors have no relations with relevant members of

Congress on the African committees of the U.S. Senate and House of Representatives.

How many African diplomats can pick up the phone right now and get Congressman Chris Smith (at home, on his cell, or in his office)? Smith represents New Jersey's 4th congressional district and is one of the biggest supporters of Africa that most people have never heard of. He also happens to be a member of the House's Committee on Foreign Affairs and chairs the Subcommittee on Africa, Global Health, and Human Rights.

African diplomats constantly complain about what the U.S. is not doing for them or their country's interests. They hire high powered lobbyist who have little ability to translate their needs into a language that is understood in the political arena. They rarely engage the American people as to why their country is important to the U.S and why they should care. They have no media strategy, no advocate within the halls of the U.S. Congress, and they lack the "friends in high places."

Africans must understand that it is important to engage the American people whether there is a crisis going on in their country or not; whether there is an adverse policy percolating through Congress or not.

The new Congress convened in January and there are many new members in both the House and the Senate who are new to their respective African committees. African diplomats have made little, if any, effort to establish relations with these new members beyond any perfunctory meet and greet.

There will most definitely be across the board budget cuts for the foreseeable future. How deep they are relative to Africa will depend on how well the African diplomatic community communicates their country's importance to the American people and relevant members of both the House and the Senate.

Based on my private conversations with members of Congress, the White House, members of civil society, and NGOs, Africa doesn't make the cut in terms of understanding how to make things happen in the U.S.

Rebranding Rwanda

Published: May 1, 2012

When the average American thinks of Rwanda, there are two thoughts that come to mind—genocide and gorillas.

During the early 1990s, Rwanda killed almost 1 million of its own people in a brazen display of ethnic cleansing. As with the Jewish Holocaust, the world stood idly by and pretended that they saw nothing!

Rwanda is also known to contain an estimated 1/3 of the world's mountain gorillas. This is the extent of the knowledge most Americans have about Rwanda. Americans are partly to blame for this lack of knowledge, but I put the biggest blame on the country of Rwanda itself.

Rwanda has a very appealing story to tell, but like most African countries, they display little understanding of the importance of engaging in direct dialogue with the American people. Better to have friends and not need them, than to need friends and not have them.

Rwanda has made tremendous progress on several fronts since the genocide of 1994. Transparency International, an anti-corruption watchdog group, has listed Rwanda as one of the least corrupt countries in Africa, they are connected to the underwater fiber optic cable off the coast of Kenya that enables them to have faster, more reliable internet connectivity, and they have been cited as one of the top 10 African countries to invest in.

Last December, U.S. Trade Representative Ron Kirk and Rwandan Minister of Trade and Industry, Francois Kanimba ratified the U.S.-Rwanda Bilateral Investment Treaty (BIT). The U.S.-Rwanda BIT was signed in Kigali in 2008 and the United States Senate unanimously approved the treaty on September 26, 2011. The treaty provides investors with legal protections that underscore the two countries' shared commitment to open investment and trade policies. These protections include non-discriminatory treatment of investors and investments; the right to freely transfer investment-related funds; prompt, adequate, and effective compensation in the event of an expropriation; freedom from specified performance requirements, such as domestic content or technology transfer requirements; and provisions to ensure transparency in governance. The treaty also gives investors in all sectors the right to bring investment disputes to neutral, international arbitration panels. USTR and the Department of State co-led the negotiation of this treaty.

The critics of Rwanda continue to site the human rights abuses by the Rwandan President, Paul Kagame (as reported by Amnesty International). The country is also criticized for its lack of a free press and the jailing or murder of those who speak out against Kagame. Most Western diplomats in the region are well aware of Kagame's alleged role in fostering conflict in and stealing minerals from the Democratic Republic of Congo.

Most Americans don't follow Rwanda enough to discern the truth about Rwanda. That's why I am puzzled that neither Kagame or his government ever interacts with the media when in the U.S., especially the Black media.

Africans constantly complain about the way Africa is portrayed in the U.S. media (war, famine, corruption), but yet they do nothing to change that portrayal. They constantly call us "brother," then they go to CNN. They tell us to "come home" (meaning come to visit Africa), but they go visit the U.S. Chamber of Commerce, the Corporate Council on Africa, or the Council on Foreign Relations (all mostly white organizations).

Can you remember the last time an African president has given a speech at a Black university, met with Black businessmen, or met with Black media?

You can substitute any other African country for Rwanda and the storyline would be the same. Rwanda and Kagame have a worthwhile story to tell, so I am dumbfounded that they don't take advantage of the interest Americans have in beginning a dialogue with Rwanda.

Can you imagine Michael Jordan hitting the game winning shot and then asking the media not to say anything? Or Barak Obama winning the presidential election and refusing to talk about his victory? Or you discovering the cure for cancer, but not wanting anyone to know?

So, my challenge to Kagame and Rwanda is to begin a dialogue with the American people beyond that of the white power structure. There are over 200 Black owned newspapers in the U.S. who would be thrilled to have an on-the-record conversation with Kagame. There are hundreds of Black owned businesses from every sector who can be a great vehicle for the sharing of ideas, but also possible investors.

If the Rwandan brand wants to move beyond the genocide and gorillas, then they must educate the American people about the progress made in their country; and the only way to do that is to begin a dialogue with the various centers of influence (COI) within the U.S.—Black media, businessmen, universities, etc.

Currently, Rwanda is viewed very negatively within the U.S. and that will be difficult to change until Kagame and his whole government decides to engage the American people. That must begin with Kagame reaching out well beyond white America that he is so accustomed to engaging with.

Kagame must set the tone, then his ministers, and finally those in the embassy here in the U.S. This type of initiative will not only help with Rwanda's political agenda, but also create more possibilities for increased investment in the country.

In marketing terms, Rwanda is a damaged brand. The only way to improve Rwanda's brand is by initiating a strategic, well thought out dialogue with the American people. Kagame has never explained to the American people why we should care about Rwanda, what Rwanda has to offer America, or why Rwanda is in America's vital national security interests. Two fundamentals in any educational campaign are: to build market awareness and then give a call to action.

Kagame has a real opportunity to show other African leaders how to engage the American people in a way that leads to more investment in and understanding of his country. An educated America is his best ally. Maybe it's time for Rwanda to rebrand it's approach to the American people.

Are African Leaders Doing Enough?

Published: September 13, 2012

I have been doing work on the continent of Africa for many, many years and to my dismay, Africa's approach to international engagement is juvenile at best and incompetent at worst. Africa's weaning from their various colonial powers began in earnest in the early 60's, so their claim of being a fledgling democracy is no longer valid. For the uninitiated, there are currently 54 countries that makeup Sub-Saharan Africa.

African leaders constantly complain to me about the way the U.S. media portrays them and how our "official" government policy towards the continent is not acceptable to them. So, I will therefore pose a few questions to my African brothers and voice a few complaints of my own.

I am in total agreement with African leaders when they complain about how the U.S. media portrays the continent. The media usually focuses on war, famine, disease, corruption, etc. You can find these same ailments in any large U.S. city, i.e. Washington, D.C. You have gang wars (to control the drug trade), people who don't have food to eat, AIDS running out of control and politicians being sent to jail. But what have these same African leaders done to address their concerns about U.S. media coverage? Absolutely nothing! They whine and complain like a crying baby waiting for mommy to pick them up in her arms to console them.

African leaders rarely, if ever, engage with the U.S. media or the American people; and they almost never engage with black media or the black community. So, to my African leaders, if you are not going to engage the America media and the American people, please stop complaining because your idle chatter has become very irritating and unbecoming of a head of state.

Africans also complain about the lack of importance Americans seem to place on Africa. Well, Mr./Ms. African president, please tell me why Americans should care about the continent or your particular country? How is your success vital to America's success? Of all of America's competing priorities, what is the rationale for us giving Africa our attention and support?

The reason most Americans lack awareness of Africa is that African leaders have not given us a reason to pay attention to Africa. I can't remember the last time an African leader actually engaged directly with the American people in a public forum (outside of New York or DC) or visited a Historically Black College and University (HBCU). They will most surely visit a white university before they would a black one.

Most Americans don't believe you can do successful business on the continent because African leaders have never shared success stories with the American people. African leaders typically come to the U.S. and meet with the usual white organizations: U.S. Chamber of Commerce, Corporate Council on Africa, etc.

The white lobbyists and law firms they hire to plan their trips never think of people like Dave Steward in St. Louis, MO (my hometown). Steward is one of the most successful businessmen in the U.S. and is black. His firm, World Wide Technology is one of the largest technology firms in the U.S. with revenues in excess of $ 5 billion U.S.

Junior Bridgeman is another top businessman. He is the second largest Wendy's franchise in the world and owns several other brands of restaurants with revenues in excess of $600 million.

Two of the most successful physicians in the state of Florida, Dr. David Abellard (Haitian) and Dr. A.K. Desai (Indian) could be invaluable in designing or expanding the healthcare system of any country on the continent. Two of the most prolific minds when it comes to understanding America's policy towards Africa are Gregory Simpkins (Professional Staff Member, U.S. House of Representatives Subcommittee on Africa, Global Health and Human Rights) and Malik Chaka (Director of Threshold Programs, Millennium Challenge Corporation)—both Black.

David Saunders and Helen Broadus, owners of Venue International Professionals, Inc. (VIP), are two of the most knowledgeable people when it comes to planning excursions to the continent. Rarely does Africa's Ministers of Tourism seek out their knowledge when trying to promote tourism to their particular country. They are also Black.

These individuals are just a few of the people in the U.S. that can bring solutions to issues facing various African countries. I am not suggesting that these African leaders give up their usual trek to their white organizations; but I am suggesting that you broaden your programs to include other American citizens and organizations that can add value to the collective goals of making Africa more relevant to the U.S. and its citizens.

So, African leaders, stop complaining and start engaging. Engage the American media, engage the American people, especially those whose roots are from the continent.

African Leaders Avoid U.S. Blacks

Published: April 8, 2013

Two weeks ago, President Obama met with three African presidents—Koroma (Sierra Leone), Sall (Senegal), Banda (Malawi), and Prime Minister of Cape Verde Jose Maria Pereira Neves. This was the White House's way of rewarding these leaders for their examples of good governance. Receiving an invitation to the White House is one of the most sought after invitations in the world, especially for foreign leaders.

African leaders constantly complain about how they are negatively portrayed in the U.S. media, about how Blacks don't invest in Africa, and about how there seems to be a disconnect between Africans and American Blacks.

My response has always been quite simple – It's your fault!

Let me break it down based on the itinerary for the delegation that met with Obama two weeks ago. In most cases, the State Department takes the lead in setting up the program for foreign leaders, but they are free to add their own program in addition to State's program if they so desire.

While in Washington, each leader participated in numerous meetings and events to strengthen bilateral cooperation on a range of shared priorities. Joint events included a dinner hosted by the Corporate Council on Africa (CCA) to discuss trade and investment opportunities with representatives from U.S. businesses; a public discussion on democratization in Africa at the United States Institute for Peace (USIP); an economic and development roundtable with U.S. government officials; and a meeting with Secretary of Defense Hagel to discuss cooperation on shared regional security and peacekeeping objectives in Africa.

Notice anything interesting here? Let me help you. Dinner hosted by CCA—mostly Fortune 500 companies (White-run companies). Many Africans accuse "corporate America" of only using Africa for their natural resources—well duh, you invited them to your country; a discussion on democracy at USIP. I have tried, to no avail, to get Howard University interested in engaging with African heads of state, but they have shown absolutely no interest. I think I can get a meeting with Obama easier than I can get a meeting with the president of Howard University.

So, I guess these African leaders couldn't find any Black NGOs to meet with or maybe their White lobbyists would not give them permission to meet with successful minority businessmen like David Steward, CEO of World Wide Technology in St. Louis–a $ 5 billion privately held firm.

Maybe their White lobbyist wouldn't give them permission to meet with the National Newspaper Publishers Association (NNPA), a federation of 200 Black-owned newspapers in the U.S., or give a speech at a Black university.

So, to my African heads of state, if you are looking for positive media coverage from the U.S., then sit with our Black media and tell them your story. If you are looking for investment in your country, then invest some time by meeting with Black businessmen when you come to our country. If you want Americans, especially Blacks to tour your countries, then take a tour of our communities when you are in the U.S. So, stop complaining and be what you are looking for.

Africa has a lot to offer as far as investment opportunities, tourism, and even education; but Africa has not made its case to the American people. Until they do, they will continue to be like the tinkling cymbal or the sounding brass, full of sound and fury, signifying nothing.

CHAPTER 6

✺ HOMOSEXUALITY ✺

INTRODUCTION BY:

Bishop Harry R. Jackson, Jr., Chairman & Founder, High Impact Leadership Coalition

I have had the privilege of working with scores of writers in the fight to keep traditional marriage safe and secure. Raynard stands out among this talented field of intellectual champions because of his

clarity, transparency, and wit.

Traditional families are the glue that keeps a society vibrant and strong; to alter that is to change the DNA of a nation. This is not about being prudish or judgmental. His stance is not based solely on his faith versus some else's faith. The U.S. Constitution, natural law, and our collective social good have been his bench marks.

I have continued to watch in amazement Raynard's steadfast belief in the importance of the traditional family unit. He has been attacked by those who disagree with him, but yet he remains true to his values

and beliefs.

Edmund Burke once said, "The only thing necessary for evil to triumph is for good men to do nothing." In that spirit, Raynard's writings are courageous. His writings are very thought provoking and he challenges you to rethink what you believe. His readers know his position on this generation's homosexual activism , but yet he has found a way to discuss this issue without being mean spirited to those who disagree with him.

I think this is what separates Raynard from most columnists—his ability to take a strong stand for what he believes, but yet invite his readers to have a conversation at the same time.

He was the only person I am aware of to defend Roland Martin from being unfairly attacked by homosexual activists when he didn't have to ("Roland Martin is not GLAAD"). This showed me that he was a true man of principle.

His column on "Heterophobia is the New Black" was a masterful piece of writing. He took a very serious issue and used a little humor to make a profound statement about the homosexual activist's social agenda.

You can disagree with some of his conclusions, but you can't deny the fact that his writings will always challenge you to examine your views-- sometimes on issues you thought were already settled in your mind.

I Won't Ask And Please Don't Tell

Published: February 4, 2010

L ast week in the president's State of the Union address, Obama reiterated his support for the total repeal of the military's "Don't Ask, Don't Tell" policy. This policy allows gays, lesbians and bisexuals to serve in the military as long as they don't reveal their sexual preferences.

Earlier this week the U.S. Senate held hearings on the issue. Secretary of Defense, Bob Gates and Chairman of the Joint Chiefs of Staff, Admiral Mike Mullens both supported its repeal. Me and my gay friends have debated this issue for years and my position is still the same, "I won't ask what your sexual preference is and please don't tell me what it is."

The gay rights movement has less to do with equal rights and more to do with acceptance of the gay lifestyle. As a U.S. citizen (and as a person), gays are already offered all sorts of protections based on existing law. That's what the Constitution and the Bill of Rights are all about. Then, there is another set of protections based on state law.

The one question none of my gay friends have ever been able to satisfactorily answer for me is why I (or the public) need to know what their sexual preference is. I like women. Strike that. I love women, but when I meet people in a social setting or in the workplace environment, I don't think my sexual preference is relevant at all. As a matter of fact, one's sexual preference is strictly a private matter and has absolutely no place in the public square.

As a heterosexual, if I talked about my sexual preference in the workplace, I could easily be reprimanded and accused of sexual harassment simply because this is a private matter and is not relevant to me performing my job. This is where my gay friends lose me—on the issue of why I need to know who they prefer to have sex with.

In my view, if the issue was about equality, then they are already protected. But, their real issue is to have their personal lifestyle choices accepted. The ultimate measure of acceptance is to have their lifestyle choices codified by law. This is their ultimate goal!

This is part of the problem with our current society. Everyone wants to have rights codified into law based strictly on their narrow interests. Everyone talks about what their rights are, but no one talks about what their responsibilities are. Rights are a direct derivative of accepting responsibility for the privilege of having these rights.

I don't have to support a person's personal lifestyle choices in order to support their right to equality under the law. Friends of mine who use drugs (cocaine, marijuana, etc.) know that I definitely do not agree with their choices, nor do I need to know when they are going to engage in such activity. Their lifestyle choices don't affect our friendship, even though in some cases it might limit it.

The gay community's only goal is to have their personal lifestyle choices validated with the force of law. I don't care what a person does in their private life, as long as it doesn't impact others. I don' understand why people insist on the public knowing the most intimate of all their personal life's details.

When I walk into a room, there is no doubt as to my race. I was born this way and God did not seek my advice when he decided to create me. Unlike me and my race, one is not born gay. They make a choice to engage in a certain lifestyle. They have every right to do so.

Some people walk into a room and you know immediately that they are gay (not all, but many). Even if they make it quite obvious that they are gay, this is not grounds to discriminate against them. I will fight to the death to defend my gay friends from this type of treatment. But, they also have to realize that our country is not perfect and with choices come consequences.

For example, there are certain upper class circles that I, as a Black man, would never take a white female to and make it obvious that we are romantically involved. Should I be able to date a white female without having to consider any negative fallout, of course; but the reality of the situation is that even in the 21st century, interracial dating is still taboo in a lot of quarters in this country. Do I have a right to date whoever I want? Yes. But, if I chose to exercise this right, I must also be willing to accept the fact that not all Americans will accept my personal lifestyle choice.

So, using the model of my gay friends, I should seek a federal law to protect interracial couples. I wasn't born to date outside of my race; it would be a choice I made. So, just because I made certain personal lifestyle choices, doesn't mean I should be afforded a special law to codify that choice.

To my gay friends, if the goal of the movement is equality; please tell me specifically how current law doesn't protect you as a U.S. citizen from discrimination. The issue of having gay marriage recognized is about acceptance, not equality. As a U.S. citizen, you are already protected from discrimination, harassment, and assault.

Therefore, to all my gay friends, let's make a deal. I won't ask you about your personal lifestyle choices and please don't tell me!

Don't Ask and I'm Telling

Published: June 17, 2010

There is a raging debate about the Democratic Party's push to end "don't ask, don't tell" (DADT) and to give amnesty to illegal immigrants. This debate provides an interesting insight into the psyche of Democrats and Republicans.

DADT is a Clinton era policy that simply says gay people can serve in the military as long as they don't make their sexual preferences known (notice I used the term preference, NOT orientation. Orientation is very passive and suggests that one had no say in the choice made, therefore the more appropriate term should be preference, since they prefer to be with the same sex). When you join the military, you sign a contract basically saying you agree to live by the rules of the military, this includes abiding by the DADT policy.

Similarly, illegals enter the U.S. with the full knowledge that they are breaking our laws, yet they want amnesty and citizenship because their motives were "pure." They were looking for a better life for them and their family.

Herein lies the fault-line between Democrats and Republicans. Democrats believe that motives/intentions justifies the means (breaking the law is ok if I am doing it to make a better life for me and my family). Republicans believe that one's action is the overriding factor—not the motivation behind the act.

So, according to the Democratic view, Hitler should be forgiven for the Holocaust because his motives were "pure." If you study Hitler's life, he actually thought he was fulfilling God's will by seeking the perfect race. Now, everyone knows his actions were wrong, but you can make an argument for forgiveness if you look at his intentions!

A Republican view doesn't even consider why Hitler did what he did. His acts were wrong—end of story.

When gays enlist in the military, they know the rules of engagement, just like illegals know they are breaking the law when they enter our country. If you don't like the law, then change the law. But don't join or engage in an activity and when the rules are enforced claim you are being discriminated against or treated unfairly.

If the rules of engagement had been changed in the middle of the game, I would be the first to fight for the fair treatment of gays in the military and illegals in this country. But, this is not the case.

If the laws are known upfront and you still decide to violate them, then I can't support demands for redress. There is nothing to redress. Either the U.S. is going to be a nation of laws or we are going to be a nation of anarchy.

DADT and amnesty are not about "civil rights." I am quite offended when people attempt to embrace these two movements on the grounds of "civil rights." I am further embarrassed and quite angered that radical, leftist groups like the N.A.A.C.P. have allowed these movements to hijack the legacy of the "civil rights" movement.

Martin Luther King did not take a bullet in his head for gay rights or illegals; and for supposed civil rights groups to prostitute King's legacy for these movements is an insult. King fought for rights based on one's humanity and being an American citizen.

King never took a position on gay rights. Gay folks are protected already by virtue of being U.S. citizens not because of their sexual preferences. Illegals are protected in this country because they are humans, but this does not extend to the privilege of citizenship.

I challenge my gay and illegal friends to prove to me that they are not already protected based on their humanity. If I assault a gay or illegal person, I will be prosecuted because they are humans, not because they are gay or illegal.

I am really getting fed up with everyone wanting special rights based on their narrow interests. So, if the Congress repeals DADT, gay couples want to get housing benefits for their partners, even though gay marriage is not recognized in the U.S. So, will this benefit apply to me, as a straight person, if I want to live with a girlfriend?

In many states, illegals qualify for instate tuition for university, but an American citizen has to pay out of state fees. Is this fair?

So, to all my gay and illegal friends, it's not that I don't like you or that I believe in discrimination; I just want fairness.

Don't ask me to accept a lifestyle I don't agree with and I'm telling you that I don't support amnesty for illegals.

I Think, Therefore I Am Not

Published: October 21, 2010

A m I the only one who has noticed the media's total irresponsible coverage of the Rutgers' college student who committed suicide when he became aware that his roommate streamed his gay sexual encounter on the internet? I think, therefore, I am not.

Supposedly, the student jumped off the George Washington Bridge after his roommate broadcast his gay sexual encounter live on the internet. The media portrayed his death as a cause célèbre as to how "gay" bullying has led to the suicide of many gay teens. As a result of this case, supporter of gay rights want laws passed making "gay" bullying a federal crime. Are you kidding me?

This student's death was not the result of him being gay, but rather a combination of factors that converged into him making the decision to take his own life.

Any psychologist will tell you that most suicides are not the result of a single factor, but a series of factors. The Rutgers' student's realization that his sexual encounter was seen on the internet may have been the last straw to his internal struggles, but was not the cause!

So, the gay community has used his death as a vehicle to advance their agenda—which is to force others to accept their lifestyle *choices*. As terrible as this case was, the issue must be viewed for what it was; a conflagration of complex circumstances that led to someone's death.

Would the public and media reaction have been any different if the same facts existed, but the sexual encounter was heterosexual? Their argument would have been that the student committed suicide, not because of his heterosexuality, but rather because his privacy had been violated and the encounter shown on the internet.

The point is that in both cases, one's sexuality (gay or straight) may have been a contributing factor, but not the only factor. The violation of privacy, in my view, is more germane than the sexuality.

Bullying has been around for time immemorial. During my childhood, I have no knowledge of any of my friends committing suicide as a result of bullying. We had fights, disagreements, and arguments. But, a few minutes later, we were all back to playing again. So, why are things any different now?

One major reason is that far too many parents are busy trying to be friends to their children, as opposed to being parents. What was it about this student's life that made him feel that killing himself was his only way out? As I stated above, suicide is a series of complex forces coming together leading to a tragic end.

We also have the grandchildren and the great grandchildren of those who came of age during the 1960s now being parents. Kids naturally look for structure in their lives during their formative years. But today's parents now give their children choices about everything. There are no absolutes. Today's kid's sexuality is more like a multiple choice exam. Little "Johnny" is asked do you want to be male, female, transgendered, bisexual, asexual, etc.? Do you want to be straight, gay, or both? Kids are told that Susie has 2 mommies or Jimmy has 2 daddies. In the immortal words of George W. Bush, "that's fuzzy math." I had a friend tell me that he has known he was gay since he was 5. I had no thoughts of anything sexual at 5, so I am somewhat confused by that.

No one should be bullied for any reason! But, at the same time, it's a part of growing up. From the media coverage of this student's death, you would think bullying is a new phenomenon. It is totally irresponsible for the media and the gay community to make a correlation where none exists. In logic, we call this a non sequitur (meaning, one's conclusion doesn't follow from the facts).

This student being gay is not why he committed suicide, but rather a series of complex issues that came together in a perfect storm. Thus, the media's argument is a non sequitur.

People need to be more critical in their thinking and not accept things at face value. We cannot count on the media or even the gay community to have a logical, thoughtful discussion of this student's death. They are more concerned about pushing a political agenda, which I find very distasteful. Because I think, I am not surprised that people are latching on to this tragedy for their own personal purposes.

Enough!!!!

Published: May 19, 2011

Rick Welts, "I'm gay." Don Lemon, "I'm gay." Will Sheridan, "I'm gay." Uhhhhhhhhhh, ENOUGH!

Who cares? Does the public really care about their sex lives? Who these people choose to be romantic with is of no concern to me and should be of no concern to those who know them.

Rick Welts is the president of the Phoenix Suns professional basketball team. He is very well respected and is considered one of the best executives in all of professional sports. Don Lemon is a weekend anchor for CNN news in Atlanta. Will Sheridan played college basketball for Rutgers University (and is now an aspiring singer).

This week each of them, independent of each other, all admitted in the media that they were gay. They were not caught in some compromising position and threatened with blackmail. They just felt the public had a "right" to know.

Here is what Lemon had to say, "I think if you're going to be in the business of news {as a reporter}, and telling people the truth, of trying to shed light in dark places, then you've got to be honest. You've got to have the same rules for yourself as you do for everyone else."

Are you kidding me? One of the supposed tenets of journalism is to report what happens and not become part of the story. What does his sexual preference have to do with his reporting on a story? So, Mr. Lemon, I want to know how much money you make, your home address, your cell and home numbers, your social security number, the name and address of your parents, etc.

Lemon is basically saying that we, the public, have a "right" to know his deepest, darkest, most private information. This is ludicrous.

I am really having a difficult time understanding why the public needs to know this. None of this information is relevant to the performance of their jobs. None of this has anything to do with workplace camaraderie. None of this is anyone's business.

This public confessional will not make them a better executive, a better anchor, or a better singer. As a matter of fact, if I admitted to a co-worker that I was a Christian (and they did not share my belief), it could be construed as workplace harassment. Just ask any human resources professional.

But, from all the media accounts of these confessionals, you would have thought they just survived the Holocaust.

Here is what former Bill Clinton aide, Keith Boykin, had to say, "Don Lemon is probably the most high profile "mainstream" black gay man alive today, and his simple act of courage will help redefine not only how society sees black gay men, but how we see ourselves." Boykin has lost his mind.

Are gays discriminated against? Sometimes. But they are protected by laws, not because they are gay, but because they are humans. That is why I am fundamentally against the "gay rights" movement.

Being gay is not and should not be a protected class, being human is. If you are assaulted, there are laws on the books that punish the perpetrator—not for hitting a gay person, but for hitting a person.

Gays who feel the need to have these public confessionals are not so much concerned about equality; but rather acceptance.

We know that the media is very liberal, thus they are trying to make heroes out of these gays who have gone public. They are not heroes, they are regular people.

Would the media react the same way to someone who publically admitted they had a drug problem, alcohol problem, or a stealing problem? Should they be portrayed as heroes too?

These are all about personal choices and the fear that public knowledge of these behaviors, in their thinking, might cause them to be frowned upon by society—thus be discriminated against.

Who you choose to be intimate with is a personal and private matter. I find it quite disturbing that gays feel the need to thrust their private proclivities upon the public.

If you choose to be gay, have at it. But, I don't have to be in agreement with your lifestyle choices; nor does it preclude us from going out to dinner or a ball game. If we are friends, we are friends because you are a nice person, not because you are a nice, gay person.

Ironically, the word gay ends with the letter "y." As in why do gays feel the public needs to know what sex they choose to be intimate with? Why do they attempt to force private, personal information into the public arena? Why do they think the public even cares about their private choices?

In the end, I don't care who they choose to be intimate with and would prefer not to be told. I won't ask, so please don't tell! Enough already.

Heterophobia is
The New Black

Published: May 7, 2013

L ast week, I had to make one of the most difficult announcements of my life—I told my family that I liked women, err, love women. Not knowing how my mother would react, I was relieved when she looked at me and said, "Boy, I knew that all along."

My brothers and sisters all said that my coming out of the shadows and announcing that I am heterosexual would not change how they felt about me and that they would stand with me when all the media requests began to come in for me to be interviewed.

I knew I was heterosexual and liked women ever since I was a small child, but I have always been afraid to come out publically because I was taught that some things are to be kept private and discussed on a need to know basis.

Now that I have come out of the closet, I hope I can get special laws passed that will allow me to walk up to women in the workplace, as well as total strangers, and let them know that I am heterosexual.

Now that I no longer have to keep my sexual preference to myself, I feel so relieved of the burden I have been carrying throughout my life.

Now that I have come out of the shadows and can be who I really am, I hope that I can become a member of the homosexual church choir that my friend belongs to, despite the stipulation that open heterosexuals are not allowed to join. If I keep my heterosexually hidden and no one finds out, I could possibly join the choir.

But why should I have to hide who I am? That is not fair and it's discriminatory. My homosexual friends want to force the Boys Scouts of America (BSA) to change its policy of not admitting homosexuals, atheists, or agnostics into the scouts; but not one of my homosexual friends are willing to join with me to fight my being excluded from their choir simply because I have publically come out as heterosexual. Anyone who doesn't accept me for being heterosexual, must be heterophobic, a bigot, and hateful.

As a businessman, I am involved with several chambers of commerces; so now that I am out of the closet, I wanted to join and have my business certified by The National Gay & Lesbian Chamber of Commerce (NGLCC) so I could become more marketable to corporate America.

According to their website: "**The NGLCC certifies lesbian, gay, bisexual, and transgender-owned businesses as Business Enterprises (LGBTBEs) and works to provide opportunities for LGBTBEs to build relationships and gain exposure within corporate procurement processes. <u>Certification</u> through the NGLCC Supplier Diversity Initiative (SDI) offers the opportunity for LGBT-owned businesses to make <u>connections</u> with America's top corporations and each other.**

By becoming certified, LGBTBEs enhance their business visibility with corporations seeking to do business with LGBT suppliers. Corporate partners can search for certified LGBTBEs through our exclusive LGBT supplier database as well as meet face-to-face with potential suppliers at NGLCC SDI matchmaking and networking events, which are held across the country throughout the year..."

I was told that I had to be homosexual in order to join. Again, per their website, the criteria for membership is: "**Is your business at least 51% owned, operated, managed, and controlled by an LGBT person, or persons who are either U.S. citizens or lawful permanent residents, exercise independence from any non-LGBT business enterprise, have its principal place of business (headquarters) in the United States, have been formed as a legal entity in the United States?**"

What I find interesting is they wouldn't tell me on the phone nor is it indicated on their website how they prove that you are homosexual, bisexual, or transgendered.

So, let me make sure I understand, they want the Boy Scouts of America to be forced to accept homosexual kids and adults; but yet, because I have come out as openly heterosexual, I can't be certified by them as an LGBT business.

This is discrimination to the highest heavens. I am considering a lawsuit against them because I think the federal courts should force them to accept me and my lifestyle choices (despite them being a private organization). I have a right to join their organization. America should stand with me in my pursuit of chamber equality.

My God, this is the 21st century and yet a heterosexual still can't join a homosexual group. I am hoping that I to, like Jason Collins (the homosexual NBA player), will get a call from President Obama. I to, hope that I can get saturated news coverage for a whole two days. I to hope Kobe Bryant, Bill Clinton, and Michelle Obama will give me a shout out on twitter.

I am brave and courageous for admitting that I like women and I think that all Americans who believe in equality should join with me for my civil rights. Where are the NAACP, the National Urban League, and the Congressional Black Caucus?

Do I not deserve dignity as much as homosexuals? I have lived my life in the shadows for far too long. Can you imagine living your whole life privately as a heterosexual? Just think of the trauma I have faced walking down the street and people not knowing if I were heterosexual or homosexual? No one should have to live their life like that. We are Americans and we are better than that.

So, I am asking Congress to launch an investigation to find out why no one is paying any attention to my coming out of the closet, why no media outlets are covering my declaration of my heterosexuality, and why homosexual groups refuse to allow me to join their organizations. How can we be the leader of the free world, but yet not give rights to heterosexuals? Our founding fathers must be rolling over in their graves.

Roland Martin Is Not GLAAD

Published: February 9, 2012

I originally had absolutely no intention of writing about the recent flap surrounding TV personality Roland Martin, but because of the unfair treatment he has received; and his seeming inability to defend himself, I feel compelled to speak out.

Martin is a syndicated newspaper columnist, a political analyst for CNN, and host of his own TV show on TV One. During last Sunday's Super Bowl, he tweeted: "Ain't no real bruhs going to H&M to buy some damn David Beckham underwear! ..If a dude at your Super Bowl party is hyped about David Beckham's H&M underwear ad, smack the sh@t out of him!" and "I bet soccer fan Piers

Morgan will be in line at H&M in the morning to get his hands on David Beckham's underwear line! LOL."

This was in reference to a TV ad with soccer star David Beckham shown wearing nothing but his underwear.

But, the Gay & Lesbian Alliance Against Defamation (better known as GLAAD) had to rear its ugly head and do what they do best—defame others! According to GLAAD's website, their mission, in part is:…."promotes understanding, increases acceptance and advance equality."

Allow me to interpret what they mean. They want to promote understanding as long as they agree with your viewpoint; increase acceptance of their lifestyle; and advance equality that provides them a "special" legal status before the law!

GLAAD's knee-jerk response to anyone who is a public figure that says anything that they disagree with is to call on that person to be fired; and then request that person meet with them. Why would anyone that you made lose their job be interested in meeting with you?

But doesn't that go against their very mission—"to promote understanding?" Isn't it more logical to call for a meeting with a person before you demand that their employer fire them? Shouldn't you dialogue with a person before you start questioning their motives and intensions, if your true goal is to "advance understanding?

In the immortal words of semanticist, S.I. Hayakawa, "meanings are in people, not in words." In short, words have no intrinsic meaning other than meanings that are internalized by each individual. For example, if I walked up to a female and told her that her dress was "stupid," she would be either flattered or insulted. If she understood the language of Hip-Hop, she would be flattered; if she didn't, then she would be insulted. "Meanings are in people, not in words."

Just as disturbing as GLAAD's demand for Martin's firing was CNN's suspension of Martin indefinitely. According to CNN, "Roland Martin's tweets were regrettable and offensive. Language that demeans is inconsistent with the values and culture of our organization, and is not tolerated. We have been giving careful consideration to this matter, and Roland will not be appearing on our air for the time being."

But most disturbing is the loud silence from within the Black community, I know first hand that many of the so-called Black "leadership" were quick to call Roland to get on his TV show or to get him to write a supportive newspaper column about one of their causes. But, now that he is in trouble not one voice is to be heard supporting him.

Jesse Jackson, Al Sharpton, Ben Jealous, Marc Morial, the Congressional Black Caucus—your silence is so loud!

They have allowed a few vociferous people to tar and feather one of their own. This is the real tragedy of this whole incident. I am totally embarrassed by the lack of courage from these Black "leaders."

Roland, you are now learning who your real friends are and they are not as many as you thought. I am totally disappointed that you even issued an apology (but we all know that CNN forced your hand on that). Do you really need the money from CNN that bad that you are willing to back away from your own innocent words? If you do, I understand. I don't like it, but I understand.

Just a side note here; why is it that GLAAD called on CNN to fire Martin, but did not make the same request from TV One, the network he has his own show on. Could it be that since TV One is a Black owned network, that somehow it is not viewed as having any value? Just a question!

Roland, remember these are the same Blacks who said absolutely nothing when Jim Clyburn was forced out of the House leadership to make room for Steny Hoyer. Again, the people he and you helped the most, said the least when you needed support

Gays don't deserve special protection because of their sexual preference, but they do deserve equal protection because of their humanity.

GLAAD talks about promoting understanding and equality and at the same time set out to destroy any public figure who disagrees with them. Roland has never done this!

I have sometimes criticized Roland for some of his liberal positions on issues, but he is a very decent person and has worked for years to bring equality to those whose voices many times go unnoticed. There are two things for sure; I am not happy and Roland Martin is not GLAAD.

Why Tom Joyner is GLAAD

Published: February 13, 2012

L ast week I wrote a column entitled, "Roland Martin Is Not GLAAD." In that column, I discussed the unfair treatment of TV personality, Roland Martin.

I thought I was finished writing about this issue and was prepared to move on. But, after receiving tons of phone calls, voicemails, and emails about Tom Joyner's "Letter to Roland: Make It Right," I feel compelled to make another comment about the Martin affair. (There are so many more important things we should be discussing, but I can't let Roland be thrown under the bus alone.)

In his letter to Roland, Joyner states in part, "his radio show's goal is to entertain and empower black people."

Oh, really? Joyner is the same person who wrote in his blog on July 1. 2011, "About a month ago, I wrote a blog about Tavis Smiley and decided to table it because I said some things I didn't want to publish. You're probably thinking I went too hard on him, but no. In reality, I hadn't gone hard enough - and I knew it. I said I'd wait until something pissed me off so bad that I would have the words harsh enough to express what I was really feeling about him and **his side piece**[emphasis added]- I mean side kick - Cornel West. Let me explain this to my non Black readers.

Remember, in my column last week I quoted linguist, S.I. Hayakawa as saying, "meanings are in people, not in words."

When Joyner called Cornel West Tavis' "side piece," it meant they were sexual partners, in other words, they were gay! GLAAD didn't utter one word when Joyner made this statement. Joyner was implying that there was something wrong with this. Where was the gay outrage at this insinuation?

Let's cut through all the clutter and get to what this debate is really all about. This has little to do with Roland Martin—he is just a convenient punching bag. This is about gays trying to force their views on society. They have not been able to do it through the law, so they just use good ole fashioned extortion and fear.

They have snookered Black ministers like Jesse Jackson and Al Sharpton into equating gay rights with Civil Rights. They have groups like the NAACP spending more time fighting for gay rights than they do for civil rights.

If this is about understanding, why do we hear so much silence? Liberal groups like the National Association of Black Journalists (NABJ) went so far as to issue a press release asking CNN to hire one of their members while Roland is on suspension! Yes, you heard right! Roland is a two time national board member and a life member of the group and as opposed to trying to support one of their own, they seek to replace Roland with one of their other members. According to NABJ's press release, "In lieu of his presence on CNN, until this matter is resolved, we encourage the network to continue to present a diverse offering of voices in its programming." Roland, with friends like these, you definitely don't need any enemies.

So, in the spirit of understanding, I have a few questions for Joyner and CNN.

Tom, in your letter, you said you were "head of the family." So, as head of the family, have you had a direct conversation with Roland since this issue surfaced? Why would you put out your statement on Friday, when Roland had already apologized and agreed to meet with GLAAD? What was the purpose of the letter after 5 days of silence? Did it really take you that long to think of a statement, or did GLAAD force your hand like the rest of the liberal Black community? You further state that Roland should make "a sincere apology." Can you tell me what that looks like? Who will decide if Roland is "sincere?" I am having a difficult time finding your apology to Tavis and Cornel for calling them gay. Can you post that on your site for us to read? Remember, you said in your letter to Roland, "the job of the offender is simply to apologize and learn a lesson about what to say or do going forward."

CNN, especially Mark Whitaker I have a few questions for you also. Whitaker is Executive Vice President and managing editor for CNN Worldwide (and is also the highest ranking Black in the network). In your statement you say, "language that demeans is inconsistent with the values and culture of our organization." Can you tell me exactly who Roland demeaned and how? Can you define for me what the values and culture of your organization is? Have you given Roland the courtesy of a direct conversation with you before the suspension? Now that Roland has agreed to meet with GLAAD, can you tell me what will determine when you put Roland back on the air?

Tom's letter to Roland was signed, "Tom Joyner." I wonder if he left the word uncle off on purpose, or maybe he just thought it would be redundant!

In many ways, Joyner and GLAAD are very similar. Both claim to seek understanding and promote equality among people, but, neither gave it to Roland Martin. So, in a way, Tom Joyner is GLAAD.

The Boy Scouts are No Longer 'Morally Straight'

Published: May 28, 2013

On my honor I will do my best

To do my duty to God and my country

and to obey the Scout Law;

To help other people at all times;

To keep myself physically strong,

mentally awake, and morally straight.

- **Boy Scout Oath**

When the Boy Scouts of America's leadership voted to allow openly homosexual kids to become Boy Scouts they, in that one act, sold their souls to the devil. Consequently, there will be hell to pay as a result of that cowardly decision.

Making matters worse, they decided to continue to enforce their policy of not allowing participation by openly homosexual adults as troop leaders. In its bylaws, the BSA has for more than 100 years precluded homosexuals, atheists, and agnostics from being involved with the Scouts. In recent years, pro-homosexual activists have increased pressure on the Scouts to rescind the policy and they won the vote with more than 60 percent of the 1,400 eligible voters supporting the new policy.

For the moment, let's remove the issue of homosexuality from this conversation and instead focus on the underlying principles – or lack of principles – involved in this debate.

According to the Scouts' vision statement, "The BSA goal is to train youth in responsible citizenship, character development, and self-reliance through participation in a wide range of outdoor activities, educational programs, and, at older age levels, career-oriented programs in partnership with community organizations. For younger members, the Scout method is part of the program to inculcate typical Scouting values such as trustworthiness, good citizenship, and outdoors skills, through a variety of activities such as camping, aquatics, and hiking."

How can you train youth in responsible citizenship, character development and self-reliance when you have adult cowards voting to shift the group's moral compass to make radical homosexuals feel good?

According to news reports, the BSA hired a polling company to gauge the level of support from kids and adult leaders within the scouts. What decent parent would allow their kid to be polled on sex and sexuality at the ripe old age of 12 or 15?

You don't give kids choices at that age, you give them direction. Kids should not be used by adults as pawns in an adult game perpetrated by radical homosexual activists.

Furthermore, when did morals, values, and beliefs become subject to the latest opinion poll or political whim? For more than 100 years, the BSA has been very clear in its position of excluding homosexuality, atheism, and agnosticism.

It is estimated that gays account for 2 percent of the U.S. population. Assuming that percentage applies to youth as well, that means the BSA has decided to make 98 percent of its troop members forsake their values in order to satisfy the incompatible demands of 2 percent?

As I predicted, less than 16 hours after the scouts changed their policy, The Secular Coalition of America issued a press release under the title: "Atheists Disappointed with Boy Scouts' Continued Discrimination Policy."

It began, "The Secular Coalition for America today said the Boy Scouts' recent decision to allow openly gay boys is a positive step in the right direction, but does not go far enough. The SCA expressed disappointment that the Boy Scouts of America (BSA) has decided to continue its policy of discrimination against atheists and gay Scout leaders. On Thursday, Boy Scouts leaders voted to open their ranks to openly gay boys for the first time. However, the Scouts' longstanding ban on atheists and gay adults remains."

Edwina Rogers, executive director of the Secular Coalition for America said the Coalition, said: "Discrimination is wrong – whether it's directed at children or adults, atheists or the religious. We will continue to encourage the Scouts to address the full range of discrimination against atheists and LGBT adults."

I happen to agree with Rogers' claim of discrimination, though not for the same reasons. The BSA's bylaws preclude three groups from participation—homosexuals, atheists, and agnostics. In order to be fair, you should not admit one of the banned groups and not the others. This is indeed rank discrimination.

Is this the lesson the BSA wants to teach our children? Do we want to say some discrimination is ok, if a large segment of the public agrees? How do you look into the eyes of our youth and for 100 years tell them that the beliefs and behavior of homosexuals, atheists, and agnostics are incompatible with Christian values and then suddenly reverse yourself and say, "Ooooops, never mind?"

Each Scout took a pledge, *"On my honor I will do my best to do my duty to God and my country."*

By walking away from its core principles, Scout leaders did not do their best – to God or our country.

Boy Scouts Shouldn't Become 'Gay Scouts'

Published: January 23, 2013

A ll that is necessary for the triumph of evil is that good men do nothing. This statement is the best way to express my thoughts and feelings about what the Boy Scouts of America (BSA) is constantly going through.

The BSA is one of the largest youth organizations in the U.S., with more than 2.7 million youth members and more than 1 million adult volunteers. It is estimated that more than 110 million Americans have been members of the BSA since in founding in 1910 (including me).

The BSA's stated goal is to train youth in responsible citizenship, character development, and self-reliance through participation in a wide range of outdoor activities, educational programs, and, at older age levels, career-oriented programs in partnership with community organizations. For younger members, the Scout method is part of the program to inculcate typical Scouting values such as trustworthiness, good citizenship, and outdoors skills, through a variety of activities such as camping, aquatics, and hiking.

I am fed up with the relentless attacks launched against the BSA by the homosexual community. The reason for the attacks? Because the BSA prohibits avowed gay and lesbian children and adults from participation, citing its principle to be "morally straight." They also do not allow atheist and agnostics to participate citing its "duty to God principle."

In 2000, the Supreme Court ruled in <u>Boy Scouts of America v. Dale</u> that Boy Scouts, and all private organizations, have the constitutionally protected right under the First Amendment of freedom of association to set membership standards. In 2004, the BSA adopted a new policy statement, including the following as a "Youth Leadership" policy:

> "Boy Scouts of America believes that homosexual conduct is inconsistent with the obligations in the Scout Oath and Scout Law to be morally straight and clean in thought, word, and deed. The conduct of youth members must be in compliance with the

Scout Oath and Law, and membership in Boy Scouts of America is contingent upon the willingness to accept Scouting's values and beliefs. Most boys join Scouting when they are 10 or 11 years old. As they continue in the program, all Scouts are expected to take leadership positions. In the unlikely event that an older boy were to hold himself out as homosexual, he would not be able to continue in a youth leadership position."

Wow, what a terrible group the BSA is. A group that actually instills values and morals into developing kids based on the principles of Christianity. These are the values that makes remote that a child reared with the values of the BSA will become a non-productive member of society. They teach children that there is a right and a wrong; there are things that are legal, but yet not moral; that the Bible is a great guiding, moral book to base one's behavior on.

As opposed to constantly trying to destroy the BSA because they have moral objections to homosexuality; why do they not start their own group to indoctrinate the youth into their desired sexual preferences?

They can call their group HIM and HERS. Homosexual Indoctrination of Males (HIM) and Homosexual Enlightenment Regarding She-males (HERS). They are free, as a private organization, to create any rules of membership they choose. And yes, they can discriminate against heterosexuals who stand for Christian values.

I am sick and tired of Christians apologizing for their beliefs. The BSA is not anti-homosexual, but is pro-Christian. I, nor should the BSA, will not apologize for my beliefs and values. I, nor should the BSA, change their values in order to make others feel good.

I find it amazing that the Human Rights Campaign (HRC) never opens their mouth when homosexuals discriminate against heterosexuals. Tonya Parker, a Black, homosexual elected judge in Dallas County, Texas, refuses to marry heterosexual couples until she can legally marry. "I do not perform them because it is not an equal application of the law. Period," she said. I guess the HRC has laryngitis when it comes to discrimination from within their community.

The homosexual agenda has little to do with the BSA, they are just a convenient target; and more to do about them forcing society to accept their personal lifestyle choices. They are free to set up any type of private club they want and indoctrinate anyone who chooses to join.

We, who believe in Christian values, have an obligation to take a principled stand in support of organizations like the BSA and not leave them to fight this battle alone.

I will be making a personal contribution to the BSA and strongly encourage you to do the same. If not us, who?

If not now, when?

Moral Only When it's Convenient

Published: March 20, 2013

As a result of Ohio's Republican Senator Rob Portman's declaration last week that he now supports homosexual marriage, I am once again compelled to ask why Christians and conservatives are constantly apologizing for what they believe.

Portman said he changed his position because his son told him that he was homosexual. Typically, I would not write about someone's family issues, as it is of no concern to me. But, in this instance, I want to come at this issue from a somewhat different slant. I want to use Portman's renunciation of his Christian beliefs to have a more broad discussion of morals and values.

Before I continue, I must tell those who don't know Portman, he is one of the most decent people you will ever meet. It's almost impossible not to like Portman. People like Portman makes me want to stay engaged in politics.

During Portman's decades of public service, he has made it perfectly clear that he is a Christian conservative, who believes in the sanctity of life and marriage being between a man and a woman.

In his editorial that he wrote last week, Portman said, "…my position on marriage for same-sex couples was rooted in my faith tradition that marriage is a sacred bond between a man and a woman. Knowing that my son is gay prompted me to consider the issue from another perspective: that of a dad who wants all three of his kids to lead happy, meaningful lives with the people they love, a blessing Jane and I have shared for 26 years.

I wrestled with how to reconcile my Christian faith with my desire for Will to have the same opportunities to pursue happiness and fulfillment as his brother and sister. Ultimately, it came down to the Bible's overarching themes of love and compassion and my belief that we are all children of God."

I am somewhat confused that Portman seems to be asserting that somehow his son can't "lead a happy, meaningful life" without his father accepting his son's personal lifestyle choice.

What makes me uncomfortable about Portman's about face is the implication that in order to love his son, he must turn his back on "my faith tradition that marriage is a sacred bond between a man and a woman." How does his son being homosexual change what the Bible has to say on this issue? Portman stated that his values where based on his Christianity—which is based on the Bible.

Since the Bible didn't change, then Portman by necessity, no longer believes in the Bible. If his daughter told him that she was pregnant and wanted to have an abortion, would he also change his view on that issue in order to show his daughter that he loves her?

One can love their family and yet be totally in disagreement with their lifestyle choices; they are not mutually exclusive. Why Portman feels the need to renounce his Christianity to accommodate his son is beyond my comprehension.

There is right and wrong; black and white; up and down. I don't have to change my morals or values to be accepting of someone with whom I disagree with.

Portman ends his editorial with, "I've thought a great deal about this issue, and like millions of Americans in recent years, I've changed my mind on the question of marriage for same-sex couples. As we strive as a nation to form a more perfect union, I believe all of our sons and daughters ought to have the same opportunity to experience the joy and stability of marriage."

Well, I, for one, am not part of the millions Americans that have renounced my Christianity to accommodate a family member. I will not apologize for my belief systems nor will I allow the pro-homosexual lobby to label me as anti-anything.

I am heterosexual, so are homosexuals willing to give up their beliefs to accommodate me? Of course we know the answer is no. So, they want me to give up my moral convictions to make them feel good, but they are not willing to make me feel good by giving up their value system. Tell me who is the real hatemonger?

Portman is doing what most parents would do—support their child; but he would be supporting his child even more by telling him that he totally disagrees with his personal lifestyle choice, but loves him anyway.

CHAPTER 7

BLACK
❦REPUBLICANS❧

INTRODUCTION BY:

Jennifer Carroll, former Lieutenant Governor of Florida.

Raynard Jackson is one of the most creative, insightful, and provocative writers I have ever known. I am thrilled to have the pleasure of calling him my friend.

I love his wit and his ability to see through the clutter and make common sense out of chaos and come up with solutions that even the proverbial "man on the street" can understand.

Raynard knows all too well the complexities of being a Black Republican. We both agree that being Black and Republican are not mutually exclusive. You really can be both. Raynard has been very critical of Black Republicans that seem to intentionally distance themselves from our community.

Though I sometimes may disagree with his columns, I am always challenged by them. He bravely writes what others only whisper in private. Raynard knows all too well that to make changes, it must be done from within. Black Republicans must collectively stand strong and challenge the Party, to take them on with a sense of purpose on issues important to the Black community. This includes having a seat at the decision making table.

I think we need more voices like Raynard's in the Party. He is not seeking to be the most popular person in the Party, but rather a voice that will praise the Party when they are right; and chastise them when they are wrong.

I think the Party would be wise to follow and pay serious attention to his writings. In his writings Raynard can be very colorful and humorous; this is his way of reaching into your psyche to make you think deeper than the emotional level.

I know he has been criticized for being a little bit outspoken, but can you honestly say that he is wrong in his outspokenness? I say no.

Any organization that wants to remain relevant must constantly be tweaked so as not to become stagnant. Raynard's columns have challenged Black Republicans to become more engaged in our Party and in our community.

The thoughts he shares in this book will empower and enlighten you. His columns are a must read for anyone who is in the political arena. Raynard, I am very proud of what you've been able to accomplish and I am proud of you for pushing the boundaries to improve the lives of others. God bless you my friend!

Being an Asset to Our Community

Published: June 11, 2013

I n the immortal words of the cartoon character Popeye the Sailorman, "That's all I can stands, and I can't stands no more."

So it is with me. If I hear of another Black Republican who gets hired as a staffer or consultant who tells their employer that they "don't want to be Black;" I am going to scream.

Let me make this perfectly clear, I will do everything in my power to make sure you never get another job or make any advancement within the Republican Party. I am thoroughly embarrassed with Blacks who harbor these types of feelings.

I am tired of getting calls from members of Congress asking me why a Black would make that type of statement to them. Many Blacks don't want their employer to call them only when there is an issue that impacts the Black community. I get that and I totally agree.

But, you need not deny your Blackness in order to work in a white world. In January of 2012, I wrote a column titled, "The Optics of Iowa." Click on the link to read it: http://politic365.com/2012/01/06/iowa-optics-where-did-all-the-black-and-brown-folks-go/.

As shown in my piece on Iowa, being Black in the context of politics is a great asset to be valued, not one that should be hid. From my Iowa piece, "...In many respects, minority operatives are more valuable to a campaign than non-minorities.

Minority operatives, in most cases, are able to work within their respective communities, but also have the added skills of being able to function within the non-minority (white) community also.

Most white operatives have no clue about how to work within various minority communities. So, minority operatives are like having an athlete who can play several positions. If money is tight, the minority operative can bring more skill sets to bear, therefore has more value to bring to a campaign."

So, by these Black Republicans telling their employer that they don't want to be typecast as a "Black" fill in the blank, the employer is now hesitant to seek the advice and guidance of this Black staffer on issues affecting their community.

Most Black Republican staffers who work for members of Congress are totally unknown to veteran political operatives like me and others; and they seem to want it that way. To my dismay, most of these staffers have absolutely no idea who paved the way for them to be on the Hill— people like Bill Coleman, Bob Brown, Sam Cornelius or Curtis Crawford, to name a few.

It's not an either or proposition; but rather, it is a both and proposition. You can be a Black Republican and work in a "non-Black" position; but yet make your being Black an asset to your member of Congress. These Black Republicans have an obligation to their bosses to avail their unique perspective on issues impacting the Black community. These staffers should also be aware that their

Blackness can and should serve them as an asset that should make them more valuable to their employer.

They also should feel an obligation to know who these Black Republican trailblazers are and to propagate their memory and legacy. They should view it as in their own self-interest to have personal relations with people like me, David Byrd, Aaron Manaigo, Mike Gunning, Shannon Reeves, Tara Wall, Tim Person, Bill Stephney, Sean Moss, Boyd Rutherford, Allegra McCullough, Patricia Ware, Kay James, Tiffany Moore and Alvin Williams to name a few.

As a graduate of Oral Roberts University, I fondly remember Oral always telling me to "go into every man's world and meet them at the point of their need." If any of these Black Republicans who are guilty of engaging in this idiotic behavior and wants to establish relations with some of the veteran operatives mentioned above, I am prepared to meet you at the point of your need.

The GOP And Black Candidates—Running To The White

Published: November 15, 2006

With the recent elections now over, Republicans are still licking their wounds and trying to figure out what happened. Well, it's not that complicated—the "Southern Strategy" has breathed its last breath.

Republicans can no longer continue to play the race card to divert the electorate's attention to superfluous issues. Even though the strategy reared its ugly head in the Harold

Ford's race, he still received 48% of the vote. Two races for governor are instructive for this.

Lynn Swann & Michael Steele's races for governor of PA & MD respectively were extensions of this strategy in a more subtle way.

Republicans wanted them to run, not because they thought they could win; but to send a signal to "white moderate independent" voters that the party is not exclusionary or insensitive to minorities. These races would also provide "racial cover" when the party decided to use their normal appeals to the bigots within the party (i.e "Harold, call me").

Then the party's white leadership (Melhman, etc.) fan out on all the radio and TV shows in shock as to why the Black community is offended. All the while, they trot out their resident Black employee (Tara Walls) to state on national TV that she saw nothing racist about the TV commercial. Ah! The "Southern Strategy" perfected.

Blacks must not continue to allow the Republican Party to use them as pawns in a bigger game of raw politics.

Implicit in the party's promise of support (both financially & organizationally) was that these campaigns would hire "their" operatives and consultants. These campaigns spent little, if any, money with minority vendors (printing, computers, office supplies, banking services, etc.), consultants, or staffing. Steele spent over $ 7 million and Swann over $ 5 million on their campaigns.

Black Republicans complain about how white Republican candidates run their campaigns, but then Black candidates do the same thing? Is it any wonder that Steele received only 25% & Swann 13% of the Black vote? It is often said that if you want to see what a person's priorities are, then look at their check book and look at who they write checks to. Using this standard, then it is quite clear that the Black vote was not a priority to either campaign.

Swann's candidacy was the ultimate exercise in ego. He had no base of support in PA nor did he have a track record of involvement in various communities. He didn't hire any Blacks until late in his campaign. All the decision making and power positions were filled by whites. Blacks want to see people who look like them and people that they can relate to. This did not happen with Swann.

Michael Steele's campaign suffered from the same flaws. All whites in decision making positions, no visible Black staffers, and no compelling message for the Black community. Steele had a story to tell, but because of those he chose to surround himself with, his story was never told. Ultimately, the blame rests with the candidate.

Neither campaign had **any** pictures of Blacks on their campaign websites, nor did either make entrepreneurship part of their campaign platform. They never made the argument as to why their candidacies were relevant to them and their business concerns.

Both campaigns were running for the "white" vote. They bought into the myth that you can't secure both blocks of voters. Therefore, they pursued what I call the minimalist approach. Their goal was to get only 20-30% of the Black vote.

This should have been an easily attainable goal if their campaigns were not run by white staffers, operatives, and consultants. As I watched their campaigns unfold, neither said anything to me as a Black that would make me pay attention to them, especially being an entrepreneur.

Their campaigns were definitely run to the "white." Their decisions, platforms, and personnel all reinforced that. Black voters neither saw nor heard anything that resonated with them. Blacks felt like they were an after-thought.

The prototype of the ideal Black Republican candidate would be Herman Cain mixed with Harold Ford, Jr. Cain grew up in abject poverty, but eventually became the owner of Godfather's Pizza, one of the largest pizza chains in the country. Though very wealthy, he has always been a very active participant in community and charitable events throughout Georgia.

On issues, Blacks have a lot in common with Republicans. But, in the words of my grandmother, "Your actions speak so loud I can't hear a damn thing you are saying." Regardless of the rhetoric coming out of the mouth of this party, their actions with their "southern strategy" overshadows their words. When all is said and done with regards to Blacks, there has been more said than done.

Michael Steele The One

Published: March 19, 2009

Michael Steele, the new head of the Republican Party, has been in office less than 50 days and he is already being set up to be the fall guy for the state of the party. On Friday, he will be criticized for the anemic fundraising numbers for March. Mind you that he became chairman on Friday, January 30 around 5:00 p.m.

He will be blamed if Republicans lose the March 31 special house election. The seat became vacant when NY governor, David Paterson (D), appointed then congressman, Kirsten Gillibrand (D) to fill the vacant senate seat of Hillary Clinton (she was picked by President Obama to become Secretary of State).

Now, let's add a little context to the picture. As with any new chairman, Steele asked for the resignation of all the employees of the Republican National Committee. During the month of February, he had his transition team do a top-down review of the entire operation of the committee and to make recommendations on how to better run the organization.

Earlier this month, Steele began to announce his senior staffers. April will probably be the first month that he will have anything resembling a full complement of senior level staffers in place. Then he has to hire staff to fill out the rest of the committee.

Now, let's talk about the real problem. The problem is not Steele (though he has made his share of unforced errors). The problem is the Republican Party! You can have the best party chairman in the world, but if the people don't like the product or service you are offering, then the support will not be there.

Conservatives represent about 30% of the Republican Party, but exercise a disproportionate amount of influence within the party. Even if all 20 million of Limbaugh's listeners voted Republican, it is not enough to win a national election.

So, when Michael made his comments about abortion in GQ magazine, he was being pragmatic. I have known Michael for close to 20 years and he has always been pro-life. But what amazes me about my more conservative friends who went apoplectic at Steele's comments is: they are quick to say that he is a party chairman who happens to be Black (not a Black party chairman). But, when it comes to ideology, these same people claim that he is a conservative chairman not a chairman who happens to be conservative. What hypocrisy. So, let's get this straight, Steele is only chairman of 30% of the party and not the remaining 70%? This is the fundamental problem with the party, either you agree with us (the 30%) on all the issues that we care about or you are not welcome in our party (the 70%).

Michael understands that he must bridge this gap in order to put together a winning coalition. That's what he was trying to say (however ineptly) in the GQ story. Most of the large contributions to the RNC come from pro-choice Republican corporate executives, not conservatives. They tend to give in smaller amounts and account for a good portion of the direct mail contributors ($ 10 and $ 20 amounts).

If the Republican Party was run like a business, it would be bankrupt. One of the keys to any business's longevity is the ability to adapt to the ever changing business climate. Like Blacks within the Democratic Party, conservatives act very emotionally sometimes and not strategic.

After the 1990 census Republicans joined with Democrats in pushing for more Black and Hispanic congressional districts, thereby guaranteeing a Republican takeover of congress in 1994. So, minorities got what they wanted but at the cost of their majority in the house and senate. Similarly with conservatives, you mention abortion and they lose their minds. As a Republican candidate, conservatives would much rather see you lose if you are not pro-life; rather than see you win if you agree with them on 80% of the issues.

When McDonald's Hamburgers open stores in China, they adjust their menu to reflect cultural differences. That's just smart business. But, Republicans would go to China and tell them they have to change their culture to fit the Republican approach to business.

Changing this mindset is going to be Michael's biggest challenge. He understands the necessity of broadening the party. As with any change, there are winners and losers. Those losers are the source of most of these anonymous quotes in the media and they are hell-bent on tarnishing Michael's reputation and weakening his support within the committee. These are the outside consultants who used affirmative action (their relationship with party insiders) to further their own business interests. Michael ended all of these contracts once he became chairman.

Now it's time to affirm Michael's actions of creating a new paradigm with fresh faces and new voices. I hope Black Republicans like Lynn Swann (ran for governor of PA), Michael Williams (currently chairman of the Texas Railroad Commission and U.S. senate candidate), will finally speak out and embrace Michaels efforts to change the face of their party. That's why I support Michael Steele!

Talking with Black Republicans is a Moving Experience

Published: April 16, 2009

Talking with Black Republicans is a moving experience---the more I talk to them, the more I want to move away! The caricature of most Black Republicans is that they are not connected with the Black community and are constantly seeking the approval of the powers that be within the party.

Well, I have been Black most of my life and would posit this question: "if Black Republicans were taken to a court of law and accused of being connected, involved and making a difference in the Black community, would there be enough evidence to convict them?"

I think the obvious answer is a resounding **NO**! The only time you see or hear Black Republicans is when they are paraded in front of the media to oppose affirmative action, oppose abortion, or oppose minority set-asides for small business. You never see or hear them talking about the problems facing Blacks in being underrepresented in various facets of American life or the problems entrepreneurs have doing business with the federal government or the private sector.

Let Jesse Jackson or Al Sharpton make an inflammatory statement and they run over each other to get to a microphone. But, when white Republicans make similar statements, you can hear a pin drop.

Of the few Blacks on Republicans staffs in the house and senate, how many interns have they given jobs to? How many Blacks have they found jobs for back in their districts or states? Can you even name any Black staffers? Do you ever see them giving speeches in the community or attending national conferences of prominent Black organizations (journalists, accountants, lawyers, MBAs, etc.)?

Why is it that Blacks like Lynn Swann (ran for governor of PA) and Michael Williams (a U.S. senate candidate and Chairman of the Texas Railroad Commission that regulates the energy industry and is one of the most powerful positions in state government) won't hire Blacks on their campaign staffs (with hiring or budgetary authority) nor spend money with Black vendors?

Let me give some advice to my fellow Black Republicans. First, STOP letting the party parade you out in front of cameras when they need someone Black to talk about the ignorant notion of "reverse discrimination!" There is no such thing. People like Ward Connerly made all of their money through affirmative action programs (under then California governor Pete Wilson), then after he cashed the checks he realized that he was now against the very program that made him wealthy. Well, Mr. Connerly, if you want to speak out against affirmative action, why not return the money you made from it, and then oppose the program.

If Black Republicans want to have credibility within their community, try to help re-integrate prisoners who have served their time adjust back into society. Work in your state to restore their voting rights (after all, they have paid their dues to society and they deserve a second chance). While attending school at Oral Roberts University, Oral would always tell me, "Go into every man's world and meet them at the point of their need." This would be a great way for Black Republicans to build credibility within their community.

Another tangible way to build credibility is to help high school students get sponsored to become congressional pages in Washington, DC. Students have to be sponsored by their congressman or senator. How many Black Republicans have ever done or even attempted to do this?

Organize Black churches to have town hall meetings with their elected officials to address issues of concern to senior citizens or veterans in the community.

Why do they not say anything about the lack of Black congressional staffers in Congress, the lack of Black congressional pages in Congress, or the lack of an agenda that's of particular concern to the Black community (lack of health care in the inner cities, the high unemployment rate within their community, the decrease in Black males going to college)?

How many Black Republicans have the personal telephone numbers (cell, home, office) to their senators, congressmen, or governors? If the public doesn't see you as having access to these decision-makers, why would they think to come to you when they need help? This is more of the fault of the Republican Party—for not publically validating Blacks who have their ear and the requisite relationship to help solve problems within their community.

The problems facing the Black community are very serious and demand more than robotic mantras that are oft repeated by Republicans---the party of Abraham Lincoln, freed the slaves, lower taxes, color-blind, etc.

As long as these Black Republicans continue to constantly tell their community what they are against (abortion, affirmative action, minority set-asides, etc.) and never speak what they are for that's relevant for their lives, then they will continue to have a "moving experience" within their community.

Michael Steele-- Chairman of the Bored

Published: May 14, 2009

Michael Steele, chairman of the Republican National Committee, is more like chairman of the bored. If committee members would spend half as much time fighting Democrats and President Obama as they spend fighting Steele, maybe the party wouldn't be in such disarray.

In all my years in this party, I have never seen any other chairman micro-managed to this extent. It is well documented that Steele got off to a rocky start, but either he is going to be chairman or he's not. If the committee doesn't have confidence in him, then vote him out. But, if he is chairman, let him operate as such and then hold him accountable for his results.

I don't think this is a racial thing, but the perception is very problematic. The public is not privy to the inner workings or discussions within the committee (and really could care less). But, I have been amazed at the number of phone calls I have received from "non-political" people asking if Republicans are doing this because Steele is Black?

Again, I don't think it's racial, but all this public fighting is creating that perception among some outside of DC.

I think this in-fighting has more to do with Steele being an outsider to the committee and his having a different vision for the party than those who are part of the "good ole boys" network within the party. It's sort of like getting in your car with your wife to go to a concert. She wants to go left at the corner and you want to go right. The destination is not in dispute—only how you want to get there.

In this case, there is no dispute that both sides want to win elections. Steele wants to go down the center of the street; the others want to take the far right lane. Ultimately, the driver should have the final say, in this case Steele (as chairman of the party).

Anyone who drives knows how irritating it is to have a back seat driver. At every turn, Steele has acceded to their directions (demands). He has decreased his media appearances, agreed to give up control of the finances, and has been forced to accept a special meeting next week.

Next week there is a previously planned state party chairmen meeting. After the regularly scheduled meeting, dissident adversaries of Steele managed to force a special meeting through a seldom used parliamentary rule. According to this party rule, 16 committee members from 16 different states can force a special meeting at any time.

Invoking this rule demonstrates the friction going on inside the committee. According to media accounts, the purpose of this special meeting is to vote on 3 resolutions:
"to urge Republican lawmakers to reject earmarks, to commend Republican lawmakers for opposing bailouts and reckless spending bills, and to label Democrats as the Democrat Socialist Party."

ARE YOU KIDDING ME?

Tell me this is a joke. They called a special meeting for this foolishness? And they wonder why they lost the election? This is a total embarrassment! This is like a college fraternity issuing a statement to the school president asking him to support higher education. It has absolutely no relevance nor meaning.

Where were these same committee members during the 8 years of the Bush administration?

To his credit, Steele vehemently opposed this foolishness, but didn't have the votes to stop the meeting from being called.

Just imagine if the committee spent this same type of energy fighting for more diversity within the party, fighting the Democratic Congress, and rebuilding the trust of the American people.

With another month spent by the committee fighting very publically with Michael Steele they have lost another month of expanding the party, regaining the trust of the American people, and sharing a Republican vision for solving the problems facing our country.

Steele should make it perfectly clear that his time and energy could be better spent electing Republicans, not being chairman of the bored!

The Voice In The Wilderness

Published: September 17, 2009

I n the week since Congressman Joe Wilson's display of ignorance, the issue of race, once again, has spun out of control. So, I will try to add some sanity to the debate.

But first, let me lay the foundation for my argument. Without question, you can disagree with President Obama without being a racist. But, what does describing Obama as a Nazi have to do with healthcare? What does calling him a liar during a joint session of Congress have to do with healthcare? How does calling him a socialist, fascist, or communist, further the healthcare debate? So, you would think that if this debate was about healthcare, the signs would read, "how will you pay for your plan, how will it be implemented, or what if I don't want your plan?"

I expect some in white America and most of those in the Republican Party, to ignore the racial nature of the attacks on the president. They suffer from cognitive dissonance, which is simply the inability to see what you don't believe.

But, I am furious and will not forgive the spineless, politically tone-deaf, weak Black Republicans for their deafening silence on this issue! Or should I say, their refusal to acknowledge the existence of race as part of the issue.

I am very troubled and disappointed in Michael Steele's characterization of this issue as "a distraction." Armstrong Williams says of South Carolina Congressman and Majority Whip, Jim Clyburn, "Some days, I just shake my head at Mr. Clyburn, because the things that come out of his mouth are more entertaining than lucid." Maybe we are seeing two different people. Clyburn rarely talks, but when he does, he is very measured and thoughtful. Remember, Clyburn is the one who told Bill Clinton to "chill" when he tried to inject race into the South Carolina primary last year.

Why do Black Republicans refuse to speak out and denounce the race baiting emanating from the Republican

Party? Saying the Democrats do the same thing is no refutation. We are supposed to be a party of principles and just because our opponents engage in certain behavior does not mean we must reciprocate. We are better than that.

It's not enough to denounce Jesse Jackson or Al Sharpton when they play the race card. Other than Colin Powell and myself, can you name another prominent Black Republican who has consistently taken principled stands on issues of race within our party?

I am embarrassed by the Black Republicans I see on the talking head shows on TV. Can someone explain to me the sign at last week's poorly attended rally in D.C.: "Bury Obamacare with Kennedy?" To add insult to injury, the signs were paid for by a Catholic, pro-life group. I guess it's OK to inflict further pain on the Kennedy family as long as it's in the name of God.

After Joe Wilson's outburst, how many Blacks did John Boehner, Eric Cantor, Mike Pence, Mitch McConnell, or Jon Kyle meet with to discuss this issue? I can tell you emphatically, **NONE!**

The Republican Party is totally tone deaf when it comes to issues of race. The Blacks they would reach out to are so out of touch with our community that they are worthless.

They are more concerned with being liked and invited to a meeting rather than making the party uncomfortable with the truth.

How can any Black not be offended and infuriated with the language and signs that refer to our president? When protesters say they want to take their country back, who is "their"? Take "their" country back from whom? That's the biggest problem with the Republican Party—they want to take our country back. We should be looking forward, but it's difficult to do that when those in the party want to go back(wards)!

Why won't Black Republicans admit the obvious? These are the whites who are terrified at the changing demographics of this country. They feel like "they" are losing control of "their" country and want to go back(wards) to the good ole days! This is the real issue.

If the issue is **ONLY** about healthcare, cap and trade, and the size of government, then why the signs of Obama as a witch doctor, him with a Hitler mustache, or with a bone in his nose?

Black Republicans need to stand up and educate the Republican Party on the way these scenes are internalized within our community specifically and the country in general. Most Black Republicans have little connection with our community, therefore they don't get the benefit of the doubt. When will Black Republicans speak out about the dearth of Blacks on Congressional staffs, at the NRSC, NRCC, the RNC, on campaign staffs?

I would love to be able to write about other issues, but I can't remain silent in the midst of such vile behavior by Republicans. The Secret Service is having fits about the security of our president and staffers at the White House are on edge every time the president leaves the building.

Now, I know how the Apostle John felt in John 1:23: "I am the voice of one crying in the wilderness, Make straight the way of the Lord, as said Isaiah the prophet."

I have been at the table in these private meetings when there were just a few Blacks in attendance. I have seen how a lot of Blacks will allow people to say very offensive things without raising any objections. So, if you, as a Black, condone this behavior towards our president or don't object to it in these meetings, you may get invited to a reception and be told that you are articulate, and a good conservative; but what do you think they really think about you when you are not at the meeting?

I am just the voice of one crying in the wilderness.

Cain Drained

Published: December 1, 2011

P residential candidate, Herman Cain, has had another trying week on the campaign trail. Those who follow my columns know that I don't usually write about issues that are salacious in nature, but, the situation with Cain has caused me to make a rare exception.

Cain's campaign has caused America to suffer from one massive "Cain Drain."

Cain's candidacy has caused America and Americans to lose their minds!

What was Cain thinking when he decided to run for president without alerting his campaign team about any possible scandals in his past?

I have worked on many campaigns in my life and the first question I ask a would be candidate is, "is there anything in your past that I should know about that is embarrassing or have you had any legal issues that I should know about?" The answers to these types of questions are part of the decision making process as to whether one should run or not.

Regardless of what you think about all the women problems Cain is having, he should never have entered the presidential race. The mere fact that he never disclosed this information to any of his campaign team goes directly to his lack of judgment. Judgment, after all, is what a presidential campaign is all about. Based on a core set of values, voters are trying to determine what type of judgments one will make as a possible president of the United States. In this regard, Cain has failed miserably!

But, Cain is not the only one to have failed miserably. The media's lack of judgment has been just as bad as Cain's. How the media can take seriously the claims of Cain's most recent female accuser, Ginger White, is mind-blowing. She has offered absolutely no proof of a 13 year sexual relationship she claims to have had with Cain. The media being shown copies of her phone bill does not prove she had a sexual relationship with Cain; it only proves Cain called her!

I thought the job of a journalist was to report the facts. So, to all my journalist friends, please tell me how you get from phone bills to proving a sexual relationship? I have several male friends that I talk to several times a day on an almost daily basis; does that prove I am having sex with them? And yes, sometimes I do get calls at 4:25 in the morning!

What do all of Cain's accusers have in common? Their allegations are all based on unsubstantiated information. None have presented any verifiably evidence to prove their allegations as credible. These women have done a major injustice to women who have legitimate claims of mistreatment. Each of Cain's accusers has been silent about their alleged involvement with Cain for a minimum of 10 years. If they have been silent for this long, it's kind of difficult for me to muster up any empathy for them now.

Doesn't it seem kind of weird that now days women will save stained dresses with bodily fluids for years, phone bills and text messages, or emails? They seem to go into relationships with the intent of securing information that can be harmful to the other person in the event that the relationship doesn't work out.

So, what do Cain, the media, and these women all have in common? They all have demonstrated a gross lack of judgment.

Because of his personal baggage, Cain should have made the judgment not to enter the presidential race. The media should have made the judgment that without hard, objective evidence, they were not going to air stories about these women's allegations. After years of silence and no verifiable evidence, these women should have made the judgment to remain silent.

Cain, please do yourself and America a favor and just end it all now because we have been "Cain drained."

Cain Was Not Able

Published: December 8, 2011

Former presidential candidate, Herman Cain, proved that despite a load of God given talent, he was unable to be a serious contender for the highest office in the land.

In the immortal words of former British Prime Minister, Winston Churchill, "to every man there comes a time when he is figuratively tapped on the shoulder and offered the chance to do a great and mighty work; unique to him and fitted to his talents; what a tragedy if that moment finds him unprepared or unqualified for the moment that could be his finest hour."

Cain, by far, was the best candidate in the Republican field in terms of oratorical skills and ability to connect with an audience. But, like Sarah Palin, he refused to take the necessary time to study the issues so he could articulate thoughtful answers to basic questions one would expect a presidential candidate to speak upon.

Cain had the innate abilities to be considered a legitimate candidate, but was not able to understand what would be required of him to be successful. He had been planning his presidential run for more than two years. But, when he received his tap on the shoulder, he decided to engage in buffoonery; as opposed to studying to show himself approved unto God, a workman that needs not to be ashamed, rightly dividing the word of truth (2 Timothy 2:15).

I literally cringed when he spoke at the National Press Club and a white person asked him to sing—and he obliged; during another speech, he went into this tirade about the Koch brothers being his "brother from another mother." The Koch brothers are 2 white billionaires who he considers a friend. These examples evoked the worst of all stereotypes about Blacks—that they are there for the amusement of their white audiences. I don't think this was intentional on Cain's part, but this is what happens when one tries too hard to please a narrow part of the electorate.

Cain is a very likable person with a very intoxicating personality. In some ways he reminds me of former president, Bill Clinton. Cain (nor Clinton) ever met a stranger. When you meet Cain, he makes you feel like an instant friend.

If you could merge Cain's personality and style with Newt Gingrich's command of policy, Obama would be toast!

Cain reminds me of a professional athlete that everyone concedes has the talent to be the best in his sport, but refuses to practice to be the best (LeBron James). This athlete could win the ultimate prize of his sport, but just won't dedicate himself to fully exploiting his God given talent.

This is why I am so disappointed in Cain. I would not have had a problem if Cain was defeated by his opponents, but I do have a problem with him losing because he was unprepared.

Cain was tapped on the shoulder and offered the chance to do a great and might work, unique to him and fitted to his talents. I find it very tragic that he was found unprepared for the moment that could have been his finest hour.

The media did not destroy Cain's campaign, nor the women who made unsubstantiated allegations. What destroyed Cain's campaign was the man in the mirror.

When Cain was tapped on the shoulder, he was found totally unprepared and proved to the world that Cain was truly not able.

CHAPTER 8

❧ PRESIDENT ❧ OBAMA AND BLACKS

INTRODUCTION BY:

Michael A. Gunning, Vice President for the Personal Insurance Federation of California (PIFC)

I first met Raynard Jackson over 25 years ago in Saint Louis, Missouri. As the one and only Black man I have known that graduated from Oral Roberts University, I was intrigued as to what type of "Brotha" he might be. Over the years I have come to know Raynard as a Black Republican "Brotha" that speaks his mind, espouses his conservative points of view and yet never forgets that he is still a Black man in America. He remembers where he came from and tries to think about how to help his community, granted from a Republican point of view.

My experience is that too often Black Republicans have no credibility in their own communities. They typically have little connection to the community and criticize Black people's behavior and do nothing to help uplift the race. Herein lies the dilemma that so many Black Republicans face – being a Republican or being Black. Too often, many Black Republicans forget they are Black in order to be more Republican. They feel like they have to be one or the other and not both.

Raynard just doesn't criticize Black Republicans, he also has been a very vocal critic of President Obama. His criticism of Obama's seeming condescension towards a community that gave him 96% & 93% of their vote in 2008 and 2012, respectively is palpable.

This is where Republicans misunderstand Raynard and his writings. In order to have credibility in the Black community, he must be seen as a principled political operative, even though his party of choice is the Republican Party.

This is a nuance that only the more sophisticated political operative will understand.

Raynard was the biggest critic of the Romney campaign's lack of engagement with the Black community during the 2012 presidential race. But, Obama had the same issues: he hired very few Blacks in positions of power, spent little money in the Black community, and rarely engaged with the Black community.

This is where Raynard derives his credibility from, his willingness to stand up for his principles, even if it means criticizing his own party.

This section on Obama and Blacks provides the Republican Party a roadmap on how they can engage with the Black community and shift the paradigm the party has with this group of voters.

For those Republicans who think Raynard has been too hard on the party; please note how hard he has been on President Obama. There can be no doubt whose side Raynard is on.

Obama's Supreme Choice

Published: May 28, 2009

President Obama's pick of judge Sonia Sotomayor was a supreme choice. I say this not for all the conventional reasons one would expect. Before I explain my position, let me establish a few facts that will give you the context for my position.

First, a president is entitled to have his nominees confirmed, unless a disqualifying issue is discovered. Disagreeing with a person on abortion, gay rights, or affirmative action are not disqualifying issues. Nonpayment of taxes, lying under oath, or not renewing one's law license, etc., are disqualifying acts.

But, as usual, expect Republicans to overreach on trying to block Obama's pick. They will further alienate independent voters who want solutions to problems and not continued partisan bickering. You can disagree with judge Sotomayor on a range of issues, as I do, but you can't make the argument that she is not qualified.

I hope and pray that Republicans won't revert back to their natural inclination of injecting race into this battle. They know they don't have the votes to block her confirmation, so they are going throw mud at her and hope that something sticks. Rush Limbaugh has already called Sotomayor a "racist." Not one Republican leader voiced any objection to Rush's race baiting.

Republicans continue to underestimate Obama's political skills. You do not come from total obscurity to being president of the United States in four years without being a shrewd and skilled political tactician. His nomination of Sotomayor was one of the most amazing political moves I have seen in all my years of being a political operative.

In Obama's calculation, he is at his most popular (his number will only go down and then stabilize), Democrats control the Senate, and he expects another pick to the court during his term. He also knows that the Republicans are in an extremely weakened position politically. They are worse than impotent right now. Therefore, now is the time to nominate his most controversial pick (on a relative scale).

Even Republicans concede that Sotomayor will be confirmed.

But, Obama's pick has less to do with the court and more to do with the Hispanic community. Obama has been under intense pressure from the Hispanic community because he has few Hispanics in his administration in any significant position. So, the president met with a group of Hispanics and promised them a town hall meeting about giving amnesty to all the illegals in the country. But, the meeting never happened and the group began to voice their frustration to the media.

After the White House's internal polling data came back and they had conversations with members of Congress, the president realized that there was no appetite to deal with amnesty this year. Word was sent to the Hispanic community to back off. So, their consolation prize was a Hispanic on the U.S. Supreme Court.

So, basically the White House's position with the Hispanic community is now, "shut up!" Obama has issues like a bad economy to deal with, two wars, North Korea, and health care, to name a few. Picking Sotomayor basically buys off the Hispanic community and will prevent them from bugging the administration about illegal immigration.

This move by the president was a stroke of genius. Regardless of your politics, you have to tip your hat to the president's move. The president knows that there is absolutely nothing the Republicans can do to counter his move. Republicans don't have anything to offer the Hispanic community.

Effectively, this is Obama's opening salvo for his reelection campaign in 2012. He has basically taken the Hispanic vote off the table. Don't be surprised if his next pick were not a Black person. If there is a third pick (which there is a real possibility), it will be a white male.

So, how do Republicans win a national election if they have written off the Black and Hispanic votes from day one? There are not enough white Republican/conservative voters to win a national election without a broader base of support.

Politically, Republicans are in bad shape and there is no light at the end of the tunnel in the near term. If the economy recovers, it's difficult to imagine a scenario for a Republican victory in 2012. Based on current political demographics, Republicans will probably lose seats in both houses of Congress during next year's congressional elections.

Obama is playing chess while the Republicans are playing checkers. That is why his picking of Sonia Sotomayor was such a supreme stroke of genius.

History Becomes Mystery

Published: December 1, 2009

In 2008, Barack Obama made history by becoming the first Black to be elected president of the United States of America. He ran the closest thing to a perfect campaign I have ever seen. But, this history has turned into a mystery since his swearing in as president back in January 2009.

Winston Churchill (former prime minister of Britain during WW II) once said, "To every man, there comes a time when he is figuratively tapped on the shoulder and offered the chance to do a great and mighty work, unique to him and fitted to his talents. What a tragedy if that moment finds him unprepared or unqualified for the moment that could be his finest hour." We all receive and experience only a few of these moments in a lifetime. How we respond to these moments will dictate our life's story.

I think Obama's candidacy for president last year was one of these moments and he responded marvelously. When he received his "tap on the shoulder," conventional wisdom told him that he was crazy! America was not ready to elect a Black man! Members of the Black political elite said, "it wasn't his time!" I, too, was one of these people.

But, fortunately, he answered his "tap on the shoulder" and went on to prove to America that he was uniquely equipped with the talents needed to win his race.

After 8 years of Bush, America was mentally and fiscally drained by the seeming arrogance of power displayed by the Bush administration. Congressional Republicans were impotent before the Bush White House and basically did whatever they were told to do.

America had been so mentally beat up—9/11, wars in Iraq & Afghanistan, partisan bickering in Congress, and the financial collapse—that they were looking for a fresh face to inspire hope in this country. So, Obama came along with a message of "hope, change we can believe in, and yes we can." He had accepted his "tap on the shoulder."

His election last November was universally received as a very historic, positive, and good thing (politics not withstanding). He took office in January with so much goodwill that he could have done pretty much anything. This is where the mystery of his presidency begins.

Regardless of what happens with his healthcare proposal (and I think he will get it passed in some form this year), this will prove to be his Achilles heel. The biggest mistake Obama made has nothing to do with the substance of his proposal. The president's biggest mistake was to allow Congress to write the bill versus submitting his own bill to Congress.

There is nothing in the president's past to indicate that he tolerates confrontation very well. This aversion to confrontation and his need to be a conciliator will marginalize his presidency if there is not a drastic change in his governing style.

No one in Congress fears opposing the president. The president needs to learn how to be more like LBJ and to crack a few heads. Democrats in Congress are much further to the left than the president. But, they seem to be crafting the agenda and the White House is just following along. Well, that's not what the American people voted for. They did not vote for Harry Reid and Nancy Pelosi. They voted for a president that would get things done, be bi-partisan where possible, and get our fiscal house in order.

Obama's election made history. But what happened to him after the election is a mystery. Where is the candidate who had no turnover in his campaign staff (this is unheard of for a national campaign)? Where is the candidate whose campaign finances were never questioned (again, unheard of)? Where is the candidate who was able to inspire all Americans that a brighter day was coming?

I am acutely aware that there is a big difference between campaigning and governing. But, this is the same person that masterfully answered his "tap on the shoulder." "What a tragedy if this moment finds him unprepared or unqualified for the moment that could be his finest hour."

Leave It To Cleaver

Published: September 22, 2010

L ast week, as I was riding the local train in Washington, DC, I began to ponder on the thoughts that had begun to flood into my mind.

I was president of my senior class at Soldan High School in St. Louis, MO. I had a lot of my friends who worked hard to get me elected. So, during this train ride, I wondered how my classmates would have responded if I decided to put all my energies into helping another school across town?

I also pondered what would happened if members of a fraternity or sorority helped elect one of their friend's as national president; and then they never showed up at any of their own meetings. But, they seemed to always find time to attend other fraternity's or sorority's meetings.

I know, I know. The thought of that happening would be unimaginable and unthinkable, right?

Wrong!

Cause that is exactly what is happening before our very eyes. Blacks are 13% of the American population and gave Obama 96 % of their vote in 2008. They are the second largest voting block in the country (behind the white population, who is 74 % of the population).

Obama has done everything in his power to ignore the Black community and finally, some of the Black community's frustration is spilling over in public. What took you so long?

As I have said in previous columns, the White House has made a political calculation that they can ignore the Black vote and suffer no consequence. "Blacks will get mad and do nothing."

While I am elated that Blacks are finally speaking out, the question is—what are they going to do? If the recent comments from members of the Congressional Black Caucus (CBC) is any indication, I am not very optimistic!

They have been quoted in several newspaper interviews ranting and raving.

John Conyers (Congressman from Michigan) said about Obama, "We want him to know that from this day forward ... we've had it... We want him to come out on our side and advocate, not to watch and wait." Or what?

No one in America fears ignoring the Black community. What are members of the CBC going to do if Obama doesn't change his approach towards them?

When the CBC kicked off their jobs tour during the August recess, Obama did the same thing-- in Iowa. That shows you how much Obama thinks of Blacks and jobs!

In the immortal words of the Doobie Brothers, from their hit song from the 70s—What a Fool Believes, "But what a fool believes he sees, no wise man has the power, to reason away. What seems to be is always better than nothing at all."

The CBC and the Black community want to believe in Obama's presidency; but there is nothing tangible he has given them to believe in. "But what a fool believes he sees, no wise man has the power to reason away. What seems to be is always better than nothing at all."

So, members of the CBC have begun to blame the Tea Party for the high unemployment rate in the Black community. People of good will within the Black community must call out these members of the CBC for what they are—race baiters. You can't blame the Tea Party for Obama ignoring his own people.

In 2009 and 2010, Obama controlled the House and the Senate. He had the votes to ram through any legislation he wanted—and he did nothing. Can you blame that on the Tea Party also?

Look at what CBC Chairman, Emanuel Cleaver (D-MO) said, "If (former President) Bill Clinton had been in the White House and had failed to address this problem, we probably would be marching on the White House...There is a less-volatile reaction in the CBC because nobody wants to do anything that would empower the people who hate the president."

I found Cleaver's statement to be extremely offensive to my sensibilities and he should have been called out on these statements. Where was Al Sharpton, Marc Morial, or Ben Jealous? Total silence.

So, let me make sure I understand Cleaver and the rest of the CBC. The Black community's agenda is predicated upon the skin color of the person in power? Because Obama is Black, he should not be criticized by other Blacks for ignoring us because we are Black?

So, in a kind of perverted way, you have the first Black president using race to hurt his own (by trying to prove to whites that he is not going to be a "Black" president); and you have the CBC using race to allow the president to get away with it (not criticizing him strictly because he is Black).

Boy, I now have a headache. So, it's ok for Blacks to use race to hurt other Blacks; but it's not ok for whites to use race to hurt Blacks?

Blacks somehow believe that by not criticizing Obama on his lack of constructive engagement with the Black community that somehow their problems are going to get dealt with through osmosis?

I guess, if you leave it to Cleaver!

"What a fool believes......"

Blacks and the Economics of Voting

Published: April 14, 2011

How long will the Black community continue to allow the Obama administration and the Democratic Party to insult them and then blame it on Obama not wanting to be perceived as a "Black" president?

Let me give an example. You have invested in a business project, Obama Inc. There were 4 classes of investors: class W, which comprised 74% of the total stock; class B, which comprised 13% of the total stock, class H, which comprised 9% of the total stock; and class G, which comprised 4% of the total stock.

How would you respond to the CEO of Obama Inc. if he says the rate of return (ROI) payout would be as follows:

those who invested in class W stocks would be paid first, followed by, class G, then class L and the last to be paid back would be class B.

Well, any sane businessman would expect to be paid by order of the largest to the smallest investor. If you were part of the class W stock (74%), you should be paid first and work your way down to the smallest investor. This is normal and logical in the world of business. Only in politics and with the Black community is this standard not adhered to.

In my above example, the class W stock represents the percentage of white voters from the 2008 presidential election (74% of the total electorate, of which Obama received 43% and McCain received 55%); the class B stock represents the percentage of Black voters from the 2008 presidential election (13% of the total electorate, of which Obama received 95% and McCain received 4%); the class H stock represents the percentage of Hispanic voters from the 2008 presidential election (9% of the total electorate, of which Obama received 67% and McCain received 31%); the class G stock represents the percentage of gay voters from the 2008 presidential election (4% of the total electorate, of which Obama received 70% and McCain received 27%).

Despite receiving 95% of the Black vote (who were the second largest shareholders in Obama Inc.), Obama has made a calculated decision to reward the gay and Hispanic communities ahead of the Black community (the smallest and second smallest shareholders in Obama Inc.). In business, the CEO (Obama) and its board of directors (the Democratic National Committee) would be sued for fraud. But Obama knows that Blacks will only complain and do nothing.

The gay community stopped giving money to Obama and the Democrats because Obama didn't deliver on any of his campaign promises to them—recognizing gay marriage, repealing "don't ask, don't tell," and giving spousal benefits to gay couples who are federal employees.

The Hispanic community threatened not to vote for Obama or the Democratic Party if they didn't get amnesty for those in the country illegally and passage of the Dream Act.

But, when asked what he would do specifically for the Black community, Obama said nothing—"he is the president of everyone and a rising tide lifts all boats!"

Despite being the second largest shareholder in Obama Inc., the Black community cannot point to a specific program or policy directed towards them and their issues. How do you justify dividend distributions to other shareholders, but not your second largest?

Privately, the supposed Black leaders like Al Sharpton, Marc Morial (Urban League), Ben Jealous (N.A.A.C.P.) all agree with me; but they don't have the guts to speak out publically because they still want to get invited to the White House and take pictures with Obama.

It took Obama almost 1 ½ years before he met with the Congressional Black Caucus; and what did they do? They got mad! Obama has yet to meet with any Black businessmen to discuss the disproportionately high unemployment rate within the Black community.

Just like no one fears angering Obama, no one fears angering the Black community. Obama has made a political calculation that there is nothing to lose by ignoring the Black community and everything to gain—including white voters!

Obama believes that if he doesn't do anything specifically for the Black community that somehow people are going to forget that he is Black.

The number 1 rule of politics is to reward your friends and punish your enemies. I didn't realize that Blacks were enemies of Obama.

The Congressional Black Caucus and Viagra—A Hard Pill To Swallow

Published: August 18, 2011

How long will the Congressional Black Caucus (CBC) continue to behave like a person who has been diagnosed with erectile dysfunction (ED) and has been prescribed Viagra by his doctor?

The male psyche is extremely fragile and when the doctor prescribes Viagra to him, initially it is a huge blow to his ego. Then, there is an initial state of denial, followed by acceptance.

So it is with the CBC and their relationship with President Obama. Obama has all but ignored the CBC and the Black community.

When Obama was elected in November of 2008, the Black community felt a great sense of joy for the history that had just been made.

After 2 years of the Obama presidency, the CBC began to think and feel what anyone with a brain had already figured out—that Obama made a political calculation that he could ignore the Black community because no one fears alienating the Black vote. According to my sources in the White House, "Blacks will only get mad, then fall in line."

Now, like a man who has been told he needs Viagra, the CBC's ego has been bruised by the willful ignoring of them and the people they represent—the Black community.

Begrudgingly, the CBC, after 3 years are exiting from their state of denial and has finally accepted the fact that President Obama has made a conscious political calculation that he can ignore them and suffer no retribution from them. The CBC has no history of punishing those who don't cater to their agenda—whatever it is.

During the kickoff of the CBC's "For the People" Jobs Initiative tour Tuesday in Detroit, Congressman Maxine Waters (D-CA) said, "We don't put pressure on the president...Let me tell you why... We don't put pressure on the president because ya'll love the president. You love the president. You're very proud to have a black man -- first time in the history of the United States of America. If we go after the president too hard, you're going after us."

Are you kidding me? Did she really say that? Yes, she said this on national TV! This is the very reason Obama can ignore the Black community with impunity—what are they going to do about his treatment of them? Absolutely nothing!

As much as I detest Obama's position regarding the Black community, I can't say that I blame him. Notice that the Hispanic and gay communities threatened, very publically, to withhold their votes and money if Obama didn't push their agendas. Blacks won't even criticize Obama, let alone threaten to withhold their votes or money.

The CBC and the Black community have become so demoralized by Obama's treatment of them that they have been prescribed "political" Viagra just to function.

Without this pill, the CBC isn't able to satisfy their constituency—the Black community. Like Viagra, the CBC can only bring temporary satisfaction to their community.

Seeing this frustration about to spill over into the public, Obama will show up at a few Black churches, have some athletes and entertainers over to the White House and continue not to offer anything specific to the Black community.

Obama will tell the Black community he needs more time, i.e. another term. But, he didn't say that to the gays or Hispanics!

So, the CBC, for the past three years, have been telling the Black community to be patient, Obama can't be seen as trying to do too much for the Black community, and don't criticize him publically because he is Black.

As a result of this, the CBC has unwittingly perpetuated the very thing they have been fighting—that no one should fear offending the Black community.

In many ways, the CBC is very similar to Viagra—if you swallow their rhetoric somebody will get screwed! And it's usually the Black community.

The Riddle of Blacks and Obama

Published: April 20, 2012

During a BBC radio address titled, "The Russian Enigma," on October 1, 1939, former British Prime Minister, Winston Churchill said, "I cannot forecast to you the action of Russia. It is a riddle, wrapped in a mystery inside an enigma; but perhaps there is a key. That key is Russian national interest."

The simple meaning behind Churchill's statement is-- something that is a puzzle or something difficult to solve. Churchill's statement sums up quite concisely, the relationship that Blacks have with Obama—an enigma.

In the 2008 presidential election, Blacks were the largest voting block for Obama (as a percentage)—96%. But, yet, the first Black president has fewer Blacks serving in his administration than former President, George W. Bush.

The first Black president thinks so little of Black women that he refused to even interview any Black female lawyers or judges for the 2 Supreme Court picks he has put on the bench. Even if he knew he would not choose them, at least interview them for the optics! Last year, in a speech to the Congressional Black Caucus (CBC), the first Black president said, "Take off your bedroom slippers, put on your marching shoes. Shake it off. Stop complaining, stop grumbling, stop crying. We are going to press on. We've got work to do, CBC."

A week earlier, Obama spoke at the Congressional Hispanic Caucus Institute. He highlighted two specific pieces of legislation that he was actively trying to pass that would overwhelmingly be to the primary benefit of the Hispanic community—the DREAM Act and comprehensive immigration reform. Not one time did he tell them to stop complaining?

A month later Obama spoke before The Human Rights Campaign, a gay rights group. Again, Obama talked about how he repealed, "don't ask, don't tell," and mandated hospital visitation rights for same sex couples. Again, not one time did he tell them to stop complaining?

Now, juxtapose that with what went on in Africa. By tradition, the head of the World Bank is always an American male and the head of the International Monetary Fund (IMF) is always a European male (until last year when the French fought for a woman to be chosen—Christine Lagarde). But Africa challenged this arrangement very publically.

Africa's actions was a direct challenge to Obama's choice of Dr. Jim Yong Kim and the brazenly unfair process the World Bank used to choose the successor of the former president of the World Bank, Robert Zoellick.

Oddly enough, Kim's strongest challenger was the Finance Minister of Nigeria, Ngozi Okonjo-Iweala, a female from a developing country. She was universally considered the best candidate in the field, even by those who supported Kim.

Russia, China and Mexico supported Kim. Ngozi was nominated by South Africa and was endorsed by all of the African members of the bank's board, The African Union, Brazil, the Economist, Colombia, The New York Times, The Financial Times, and 39 former senior officials at the World Bank.

This is the first time in the history of the bank that the U.S. has been challenged by developing and emerging countries. South African Finance Minister, Pravin Gordhan, went so far as to say, "the bank's selection process falls short and is not transparent or merit-based.

Wow! The first Black president, with African roots is being criticized by another African for not supporting the best qualified candidate for the job. Obama promised to make his administration the most ethical, transparent administration in history. But, like in many of his actions, when he had the chance to turn his rhetoric into action, he became like sounding brass or the tingling cymbal; full of sound and fury, signifying nothing.

As a result of Jesse Jackson's unsuccessful presidential bids in 1984 and 1988, he made it possible to believe that a Black could one day become president of the U.S; so has Ngozi Okonjo-Iweala's bid to become president of the World Bank. She did not win, but now other countries can envision a time in the not too distant future, that the head of the World Bank will be a non-American.

You had an African woman to challenge Obama's choice to lead the bank; she being universally considered the best qualified for the job. But, yet Black Democrats in America refuse to challenge the first Black president when he has gone out of his way to ignore them when it comes to legislation of particular interest to them. They continue to make excuses for his lack of action—he needs more time, the President can't undo in 4 years what took Bush 8 years to create or he will pay attention to us in his second term.

The Black community's behavior is a riddle, wrapped in a mystery inside an enigma.

Holding President Obama Accountable

Published: January 25, 2013

Four years ago, President Obama made history by becoming the first Black president in the history of the U.S. I would like to think that even those who did not support his candidacy was proud of what the American people demonstrated---that anything is possible within our system of government. Play by the rules, work hard, present a compelling agenda and the American people will respond.

Obama was by far a much better candidate than John McCain and presented a more inspiring vision for America. McCain had much more substance, but an inability to speak directly to the American people.

Four years later, "Hope and Change" has turned in to "I Hope He Changes." This is a common sentiment running through the Black community. They were disappointed in the total silence of the Obama administration's on issues like the high unemployment rate within the Black community; the lack of engagement within the continent of Africa; and the seeming lack of attention paid to domestic issues.

I will remind you that Blacks gave Obama 96% of their vote in 2008 and thus far has little to show for it. Homosexuals (2% of the electorate has seen tangible results from Obama—repeal of Don't Ask Don't Tell; the push to recognize homosexual marriage, etc.), illegals have seen tangible results from Obama (the push for amnesty, the Dream Act, etc.), but Blacks have seen and heard speeches—"get out of bed, put your marching shoes on and stop complaining."

So, the question I have been pondering is this: which is more important to the Black community—someone who makes them feel good (Obama) or someone who secures tangible legislation to address their concerns?

Psychologically speaking, no one can make you feel good if you don't already feel good about yourself. No one can make you feel loved if you don't already love yourself. You never hear homosexuals or illegals speaking in terms of

Obama making them feel good. They want something specific or they are willing to withhold their support.

I think there is strong consensus within the Black community that the unemployment rate is at epidemic proportions and would not be tolerated within other communities; but we have shown no willingness to do anything about it other than complain.

Remember former Chairman of the Congressional Black Caucus once said that "if Obama was white, we would be marching on the White House." So, why should any person take the Black community seriously when there is no fear of retribution? Was it not LBJ who said, "Better to be feared than to be loved?"

But, I am curious as to how we can have one standard for a Black president and another one for a white one? Should we not be marching on the White House regardless of color, if Black unemployment is double digits? Should we not be marching on the White House when over 500 Blacks have been killed in Chicago (and many of them young children) and a sitting president barely mentions it publically? Should we not be marching on the White House when our president is rebuilding countries all over the world, while ours is falling apart?

I, like most Americans, was thrilled to see a Black person elected president. But, I can't get a job based on a feeling, I can't get a student loan because I feel good, I can't prevent crime from happening because I feel good. At some point you must take away the emotional (feeling good) and replace that with something tangible (legislation).

Our presidents represent the whole of the U.S., but sometimes different groups need special attention based on their unique needs. This is one area where Obama has been grossly derelict. But, again, what are Blacks prepared to do to get him to act? Thus far, the answer has been absolutely nothing.

So, in a kind of weird way, Obama has made it much easier for future white presidents to ignore Blacks, regardless of party. For example, we know the next president will be white, so what happens when he doesn't do something Blacks think he should and his response is, "you didn't ask Obama for this, so why should I do it for you? This is strictly a hypothetical question, but I can guarantee that future presidents and their staffs will at least think these thoughts. How does the Black community deal with this question?

This is the problems Blacks have created for themselves by giving Obama a pass on many issues simply because he is Black. We must become more politically sophisticated and less emotional. Despite the historic nature of his presidency, his lack of a real relationship with the Black community is a mystery.

Black Leaders Have Sold Out

Published: April 25, 2013

Once again the Black community has been shown how irrelevant they have become in the U.S. Most of the blame can be laid at the feet of the media appointed Black leadership for selling out their people for free. Yes, for free. At least Judas Iscariot had the sense enough to get 30 pieces of silver when he sold out Jesus Christ.

Isn't it amazing that with all the debate swirling around the issue of amnesty for the illegals in the U.S., no one on either side of the debate has engaged with the Black community? Blacks will be hurt the most by giving amnesty to these 11 million illegals and yet there has not been one town hall meeting with the Black community to discuss this issue and how it will negatively impact the Black community's high unemployment rate.

No one disputes the disproportionately high unemployment rate within the Black community—about 15%. If the white community had the same unemployment number, it would be declared a national emergency and Congress would be having hearings all over the country to solve this problem.

So, why do liberal Black groups like the NAACP, the National Urban League, and the Congressional Black Caucus put so much energy in support of homosexual marriage and amnesty for illegals? These groups all acknowledge the high unemployment rate in the Black community is at an epidemic level; but their solution is to increase competition for the few low and unskilled jobs, in which Blacks are disproportionately represented.

So the media trots out Ben Jealous, Marc Morial, Marcia Fudge, and Al Sharpton to provide political cover for a policy that will further devastate the Black community. These folks do not represent the Black community, they represent the Democratic Party. In most cases, the Black community's interest is not the same as the Democratic Party's interests. Jealous, Morial, Fudge, and Sharpton are more concerned with getting invited to a party so they can take a picture with Obama or Pelosi.

Why is it that these media appointed Blacks always take up other group's causes to the detriment of the people they claim to represent?

Where was the illegal Hispanic community on Trayvon Martin? Where was the homosexual community on Apartheid in South Africa or the genocide in Rwanda? Where are the white women on repealing the "wet foot, dry foot policy" in Miami?

None of these groups have stood with Blacks enmass on any of these issues; but yet Blacks lose their minds to support them on the issues they care about—homosexual marriage, amnesty for illegals, and including women in affirmative action.

The rank and file in the Black community is totally against amnesty for illegals, marriage for homosexuals, etc. So, to my many readers, don't believe all the bogus polls about how America supports amnesty for these illegals—because they don't. Remember, these are the same polls that said the criminal background check bill would past the Senate last week.

Can somebody please explain to me how the media touts polls that say 65% of Americans support homosexual marriage; but yet 30 states have laws on the books that define marriage as between a man and a woman? The math doesn't add up.

So, as it was with the defeat of the criminal background check bill before the Senate last week, the amnesty bill submitted in the Senate will similarly be defeated. The liberal media and their appointed Black mouthpieces will be totally discredited upon the defeat of this amnesty bill and I predict that many of them will no longer be running their respective organization afterwards because they are so out of touch with the Black community.

These are some of the issues that the Republican Party can engage with the Black community on and win new allies in the fight to bring them into the party. I challenge Eric Cantor to do a series of town-hall meetings within the Black community on these issues of illegal immigration, homosexual marriage, and values in general.

Even within the Republican Party, there are varying positions on these issues; but the point of the town-halls is to show that there are many opinions within the Black community on these issues. Most Blacks are not liberal on these issues, but as I have often said, Republicans never engage the Black community even when they agree with the party on certain issues. As Reagan once told me, "my 80% friend is not my 20% enemy."

If the party deals with some of these issues, then we might be able to say, "My 93% enemy can become my 20% friend."

ABOUT THE AUTHOR

Raynard is a native of St. Louis, MO. He attended Lowell and Hamilton grade schools and graduated from Soldan High. He then went on to receive his Bachelors of Science degree in Accounting from Oral Roberts University in Tulsa, OK.

Upon returning to St. Louis, he worked in corporate America and become involved in Republican politics, ultimately being asked by the Bush family to help lead the presidential campaign of then Vice President George H.W. Bush in 1988.

As a result of being part of the successful Bush campaign, he relocated to Washington, DC. He continued his work in the accounting profession while furthering his political activities.

He also received his Master of Arts in International Business from George Mason University in Fairfax, VA.

He is a sought after political commentator and can be seen on CNN, MSNBC, BET, TV ONE, FOX News Channel, etc.

He is a former nationally recognized, awarded winning, syndicated radio talk show host and is a current nationally syndicated newspaper columnist. He is syndicated by the

National Newspaper Publishers Association to over 200 newspapers every week.